A KID'S GAME PLAN FOR GREAT CHOICES

FOR

AN ALL-SPORTS DEVOTIONAL

MICHAEL
ROSS

CHRISTOPHER
ROSS

HARVEST
Kids™

HARVEST HOUSE PUBLISHERS
EUGENE, OREGON

Cover design by Left Coast Design

Cover illustration by Krieg Barrie

Published in association with WordServe Literary Group, Ltd., www.wordserveliterary.com.

HARVEST KIDS is a trademark of The Hawkins Children's LLC. Harvest House Publishers, Inc., is the exclusive licensee of the trademark HARVEST KIDS.

A Kid's Game Plan for Great Choices
Copyright © 2019 by Michael Ross and Christopher Ross
Published by Harvest House Publishers
Eugene, Oregon 97408
www.harvesthousepublishers.com

ISBN 978-0-7369-7524-7 (pbk.)
ISBN 978-0-7369-7525-4 (eBook)

Library of Congress Cataloging-in-Publication Data

Names: Ross, Michael, 1961- author. | Ross, Christopher, 2002- author.
Title: A kid's game plan for great choices / Michael Ross and Christopher
    Ross.
Description: Eugene, Oregon : Harvest House Publishers, [2018]
Identifiers: LCCN 2018026611 (print) | LCCN 2018040559 (ebook) | ISBN
    9780736975254 (ebook) | ISBN 9780736975247 (pbk.) | ISBN 9780736975254
    (ebk.)
Subjects: LCSH: Christian children--Conduct of life--Juvenile literature. |
    Christian teenagers--Conduct of life--Juvenile literature. |
    Sports--Religious aspects--Christianity--Juvenile literature.
Classification: LCC BV4571.3 (ebook) | LCC BV4571.3 .R673 2018 (print) | DDC
    305.235088/27--dc23
LC record available at https://lccn.loc.gov/2018026611

Printed in the United States of America

18 19 20 21 22 23 24 25 26 / BP-SK / 10 9 8 7 6 5 4 3 2 1

To Debbie and Will Smith

Your friendship, support,
and inspiration mean everything.

SCRIPTURE PERMISSIONS

Contents

PART 3: WINNING WITH YOUR CLASS
A Game Plan for A+ Encounters with Classmates and Teachers

PART 4: WINNING WITH FAMILY

A Game Plan for Scoring BIG with Parents and Siblings

Starting Point
Play like a Pro, Live like a Leader

STEPHEN CURRY—A WARRIOR
AND A CHAMPION

The game is in overtime with just 20 seconds on the clock. The ball passes to No. 30—a young MVP known worldwide as the greatest shooter in NBA history. And today, Stephen Curry lives up to that reputation.

In one continuous motion, he grabs the ball and then releases it. A beautiful orange streak arcs through the air as the clock ticks down. *SWISH*…right on the buzzer!

The crowd roars, and the Golden State Warriors pick up another win.

Curry high-fives his teammates and points his index finger toward the sky. He quickly gives credit to the source of his abilities—and the very key to winning in life: "I can do all things through Christ who strengthens me" (Philippians 4:13 NKJV).

ALLYSON FELIX—ON A FAST
TRACK TO GREATNESS

The runner who was labeled "Chicken Legs" in high school—because of her lanky physique—now stands proudly on an Olympic platform with a gold medal dangling around her neck.

Cameras flash, the national anthem plays, and a sea of fans chant her name.

But Allyson Felix doesn't stop with just one victory. She goes on to win nine Olympic medals, six gold and three silver, making her the most decorated woman in US track and field history. "I'm always nervous," Felix admits. "If I wasn't nervous, it would be weird. I get the same feeling at all the big races. It's part of the routine, and I accept it. It means I'm there, and I'm ready."

Yet it's her faith in God that helps her beat the jitters, face the competition…and win in life, not just on the track. "The most important lesson that I have learned is to trust God in every circumstance," Felix says. "Lots of times we go through different trials. And sometimes following God's plan seems like it doesn't make sense at all. But I know that God is always in control. He will never leave us."[1]

MARK SANCHEZ—THE NFL'S COOL QB POWERHOUSE

Mark Sanchez heads into his eighth season in the NFL, suiting up for the Chicago Bears as the backup to quarterback Mike Glennon. While Sanchez doesn't get to own the spotlight, this veteran QB knows he's serving a valuable role as a mentor. He gets to share his abilities with less experienced players.

Dallas rookie quarterback Dak Prescott is one of those guys. Prescott credits Sanchez for helping him learn how to be a professional.

"My dad always told me that if you want to be successful, you hang around people who are successful," Sanchez says. "If you want to be a good Christ-follower, be around people who will disciple you. I try to surround myself with people who will strengthen and challenge me in my faith and on the field. I try to do the same for others."

For Sanchez, playing like a pro means living like a leader. And both take obedience.

"If you love God, how do you show your love for Him?" he asks. "There's no material thing you can give back. He's already done everything for you, so you obey. That's how you love God. So how do you love your neighbor? You help them love God."[2]

Three athletes. Three very different stories. One rock-solid faith.

Curry, Felix, and Sanchez share an intense drive to win and a passion to push themselves and to excel under pressure. But they don't live for trophies and titles, and showboating for their fans isn't their style either. These athletes compete for something—*Someone!*—much greater than themselves. They share a purpose that makes them true champions. What is it?

They're committed to knowing, loving, and following Jesus Christ.

They're committed to obeying what God's Word teaches.

They're committed to a game plan that leads to an eternal prize.

> "All athletes are disciplined in their training. They do it to win a prize that will fade away, but we do it for an eternal prize. So I run with purpose in every step. I am not just shadow-boxing. I discipline my body like an athlete, training it to do what it should" (1 Corinthians 9:25-27 NLT).

I want that eternal prize.

And just like my sports heroes, I want to win in life, not just in the game.

I'm Christopher, a basketball-shootin', lacrosse-playin', football kickin', competition-crazed kid...and the cocreator of this book. Yep, that's my name on the cover—right next to my dad's. (Pretty cool for a 16-year-old, huh?)

I'm learning all kinds of cool stuff that's helping my faith to grow—like how to pray and read my Bible. I'm making better choices too—in my virtual worlds (music and gaming), with the team, at school, and at home—and I can't wait to share everything with you.

But be warned: The contents of this *A Kid's Game Plan for Great Choices* is highly contagious! I guarantee you'll never be the same as you fill your brain and heart with all the stories, stats, verses, and advice packed into these pages. You'll uncover the secrets to life as you discover some really cool stuff about God!

So let's get started with one more athlete profile...mine!

CHRISTOPHER ROSS—A YOUNG HOOPSTER WITH HEART

THUNK, THUNK, THUNK...SWOOSH!

Another three-pointer for the visiting team. I glance at the scoreboard and groan. *Twenty-six to zero? They're killing us!*

My team's chances of winning the regional tourney and becoming middle-school champs just slipped away—which doesn't make sense to me.

Earlier that day, we owned the court. Just a couple of hours ago, we could taste victory. The fist bumps were bumping, my friends cheering, and my confidence soaring. *We* were the favored players.

"Excellent teamwork," the coach told everyone. "You won because you played like champions. You worked together, ran the plays, passed the ball, and really hustled out there. Most of all, you played hard until the clock ran out. I'm proud of each one of you."

But now? Our hopes of winning are gone.

It's as if we've forgotten everything the coach has taught us—every drill, every tactic. Suddenly, we're falling apart.

I look up again at the giant zero glaring down from the scoreboard. *That's how I feel right now*, I tell myself. *Champions? Not us. Not today.*

But then I notice the coach on the sidelines. He isn't pacing or slamming his clipboard on the ground. He's just standing there, calmly observing. His eye catches mine, and he gives me a thumbs-up.

What? Can't he see the scoreboard? I ask myself in disbelief. *Everything's going wrong, and he's not mad?*

And then I recall something he told me: "Character, commitment, *heart*—that's what I see in you, and believe me, that's what separates a mere player from a real champion. Sometimes we win, sometimes we lose…but it's a Christ-centered heart that guides us through trials."

Okay—I'll keep it together. I'll play like a champ—no matter what happens.

"God's Spirit makes us loving, happy, peaceful, patient,
kind, good, faithful, gentle, and self-controlled"
(Galatians 5:22-23 CEV).

Postgame update: We lost this competition but came in third place in the tournament. According to our coach, "Our game play made us the true champions! We had the right attitude.

Now it's your turn. Fill out your very own all-star stats on the next page.

MY ALL-STAR STATS

_____

(Print your name here)

_____

(Add your sport and the position you play)

Write about your own game play.

A big win or a crushing loss.

_____

_____

_____

_____

Jot a few lines about your favorite pro athlete.

What makes this athlete special?

_____

_____

_____

_____

Share the best advice you've ever received— for the game and for real life.

Who said it, and how did it help you?

_____

_____

_____

_____

You'll find "My All-Star Stats" in each section of the book. This is your journal space—a place to jot down what you're thinking and feeling, a place to record the most important tactics for winning in the game…and especially in life.

TACTICS YOU'LL LEARN

A Kid's Game Plan for Great Choices is all about peer-to-peer connections. It's written through my eyes—and I'm a sports-crazed kid like you! Within these pages are stories from my world, kid-relevant lessons that bring to life Bible verses, and tons of pro tips about making good choices.

You'll find 40 devotions divided among four topics:

- Winning with Friends: A Game Plan for Championship Connections

- Winning with the Team: A Game Plan for Godly Sportsmanship

- Winning with Your Class: A Game Plan for A+ Encounters with Classmates and Teachers

- Winning with Family: A Game Plan for Scoring BIG with Parents and Siblings

This fast, fun book tackles what matters most to us.

As you step into my world, meet my friends, and hear from the pro athletes we admire, we'll begin to think about our choices in life and clue in to an important truth: The paths we set foot on, the friends we associate with, and the way we choose to spend our time affect our lives and our friends' lives…for all eternity.

Let's head to the court…or field, or gym, or pool (wherever you like to compete). It's time for some intense training. It's time to win!

Part 1

Winning with Friends

A Game Plan for Championship Connections

1

Let the Cybergames Begin

The battle is on.

SMASH…CRUNCH!

Ouch! My Arena Tower was hit but not taken down. I've deployed my troops, and I'm going after the King's Tower in my opponent's territory.

An "emote" pops up with a message from the enemy. (Emotes are short comments that can be accessed by the speech bubble icon.) This one is an emoji with a laughing king face.

He's taunting me, I tell myself.

I fire off my own emote: "You're goin' down!"

My warriors surround the tower and move in for a win. Can we succeed? Will my clan rule the day? In this competition, anything is possible.

I'm on my cell phone playing *Clash Royale*. It's a "freemium" tower-defense game that pits players against other real-world opponents, and it all takes place in a medieval cartoon world. The graphics are bright, simple, and pretty cool…and the action is thrilling. But the more I play, the more annoyed I become.

It's tough to succeed in this game without two things: patience and real-world money.

Rewards and upgrades require either lots of time or cash to unlock. (And I've already used up my allowance.) There's also an in-game chat function that lets players communicate directly with one another, and the guys I'm up against are swearing a lot. They're even sharing personal information. Those are two things I don't do.

Should I keep playing? I ask myself. *Hmmm…I won't quit just yet. One more battle.*

I quickly learn that players need super fast reaction times, and they have to come up with dozens of different strategies for many possible situations. That's all good. I like to be challenged and to solve problems under pressure. (It brings out my competitive side.) And I notice that with an amazing strategy, a level-two player can defeat a level-six competitor.

But then things go downhill again.

Players try to acquire seven legendary cards. But they come with a price: They cost real-world money, and they aren't cheap. Most high-level players rely on these cards, which give them an unfair advantage. Like I said, I've used up my allowance…so I'm at a huge disadvantage. My strategies are good, but I can't play if I can't pay. And that's so frustrating.

I notice something else: The longer I play this game, the harder it is for me to win…and to quit. There seems to be an addictive element. I'm serious!

Also, the system matches players with similar skills and styles. So if I play crazily, I'll be matched with other crazy players. Pretty smart thinking by the game makers…and yet another appealing feature of this game. But along with the good is the bad.

It's easy to get lost for hours in game play…and end up in a really bad mood.

Suddenly, more swearing from other players.

"That's it!" I say out loud. "Game over."

CLICK.

I love gaming with my friends. It's how a lot of kids socialize these days. Computers and the web keep us connected, and they are powerful tools—so powerful they can eat us alive if we don't watch out. Let's not give them a chance. The key: Stop acting like babies, not knowing right from wrong, constantly letting down our defenses in our cyberworlds, and getting pulled into dangerous traps.

It's time to grow up spiritually. Kids our age need to know how to make good choices.

WINNING WORDS

"People who live on milk are like babies who don't really know what is right. Solid food is for mature people who have been trained to know right from wrong" (Hebrews 5:13-14 CEV).

WINNING TACTICS

- *Honor Mom and Dad.* If we're serious about keeping our minds clean and our hearts pure, we need to get serious about accountability. Be open with your parents about your gaming and online activities. Remember, sin loves privacy and hates light. (See Isaiah 29:15.)

- *Have more face-to-face time with your friends*…and consider limiting game time and other activities online. This keeps us from becoming addicted to our favorite pastimes, and it reduces the chance of getting into trouble in our high-tech hangouts.

- *Never talk to strangers.* We're growing up with the "internet of things," and we're well aware that social network sites attract thousands of people. Some of them who play on kid-friendly games like *Minecraft* aren't kids. And some are dangerous. Be smart by playing smart. Never, ever talk to people you don't know.

Read Psalm 111:10. What leads to wisdom and helps us make good choices?

2

Hanging Out
(Just the Basics)

Jason yanked the hamburger out of Kyle's hand and took a bite. "Go on—talk to her for me," he mumbled while chewing, then opened his mouth and exposed the contents.

"*Gross!* You just ruined my lunch," Kyle said. "Look—you're the star forward everyone likes...so *you* talk to her."

Eric slammed his math book on Kyle's fries—*WHAM!*—and scraped the remains into a nearby trash can. "*That's* what I call gross," he said with a grin. "Almost as gross as your goalie skills."

"You're history," Kyle snapped. "I'm going to rip your—"

The guys froze in their tracks. "Girl alert," Eric blurted.

Two of their school's nicest girls walked by. One of them was the amazing forward on the girls' soccer team. Jason sort of had a crush on her. (Only *sort of.*)

Jason grabbed Kyle by the shoulders. "Please, Kyle, you've got to help us!"

"No way," Kyle snapped. "With you rejects around, I'm not going anywhere near those girls!"

"But they talk to you."

"And with your help, they might even talk to us," Eric added.

"I'd rather have my tongue cut out."

"You're my best friend," Jason pleaded.

"Friends help each other," Eric interjected.

"They don't destroy a guy's lunch."

Jason held up a french fry. "My last one. Take it."

Kyle's eyes lit up. A grin slowly formed on his lips. He flicked a french fry off Eric's book and then fist-bumped Jason. "Deal!"

Lisa's face grew red as Heather filled her in on the latest gossip from Shelly.

"I can't stand her," Lisa exploded as she shoved another potato chip into her mouth. Everyone had invaded Niki's house after practice for some snacks and girl time.

"I can't believe she's spreading those lies," Lisa continued. "I'm so mad at Shelly, I could strangle her, and I think I would if I had the chance."

"And I thought you two were best friends," Niki said.

"Yeah, girl," Heather interjected. "Aren't you, like, twins? We don't see one without the other."

Lisa practically choked on her chips. "Us…best friends? More like frenemies."

"It's 4:45," Niki's mom yelled down to the basement. "Time to go."

The "Mom alarm" sent Lisa and Heather off to their own homes.

On her way down the street, Lisa was fuming. *How dare that Shelly?* Lisa thought. *She may be Miss Cheerleader, well liked and everything…but just who does she think she is?*

Lisa picked up her pace, shot around the corner, and then stopped.

"Hey there, Lisa," Shelly squeaked, throwing her arms around Lisa.

"Oh, uh…hi, Shelly." Lisa flashed a grin and then brushed her hair out of her eyes. "So uh, how's my…friend doing today?"

"Couldn't be better." Shelly pressed closer to Lisa. "Hey, have I got some juicy news about Heather. Come by my house later, okay? Let's invite a few of the girls over. We'll have a great time!"

"Ah, sure…later…with a few *friends*. Wouldn't miss it!"

This is *friendship*?

Hanging out with the Three Stooges at a toxic waste dump would be less hazardous. Sometimes friends treat each other more like enemies than friends.

I know because my friends are crazy. Leave it to them to do dumb things at the worst possible moments.

Guys: Our friends belch around girls, pull pranks that aren't funny, and spill soda all over our new basketball shoes—then blame it on someone else.

Girls: Your friends blab secrets when they shouldn't, make you feel like crawling into the nearest hole as they embarrass you, and sometimes make you wonder if being a hermit isn't such a bad option.

As for me, I wouldn't have it any other way—and I bet you wouldn't either. We take a few jabs and risk some bruises now and then because friendship is important.

When push comes to shove, my friends stick with me better than the gooiest slice of pepperoni pizza. My buddies also help me beat boredom—they're good for more laughs (and screams) than the world's fastest triple-looping roller coaster. And even if I don't realize it, they help me grow and learn more about myself. Sometimes the only way to figure out what we're really thinking or feeling is to talk things out with a friend. And when we're with our friends, we can be ourselves. It doesn't matter if we drool or have big wads of gum stuck in our ears. True friends accept us just the way we are.

So what are good choices and bad ones when it comes to hanging out? I have some ideas.

WINNING WORDS

"Here is my command. Love one another, just as I have loved you. No one has greater love than the one who gives their life for their friends. You are my friends if you do what I command. I do not call you slaves anymore. Slaves do not know their master's business. Instead, I have called you friends. I have told you everything I learned from my Father" (John 15:12-15).

WINNING TACTICS

- *Choose friends, not phonies.* God wants us to have friends—guys and girls to hang out with, to share great experiences with, to laugh with. But He knows that friendships aren't always smooth sailing, so He wants us to choose our friends carefully. True friends don't laugh at our imperfections. They accept us just the way we are, stay by our sides through thick and thin, stick up for us...and can be trusted. A phony, on the other hand, constantly puts us down, tries to turn us into something we're not, takes off when the going gets rough, lies to our faces, and stabs us in the back.

- *Choose friends who are positive influences.* The people we hang out with can have a big impact on our lives. "Don't fool yourselves. Bad friends will destroy you" (1 Corinthians 15:33 CEV). Ask yourself an important question: *Is this friend dragging me down?*

- *Choose friends the way Jesus did.* He gathered a group of people around Him who had the potential to change the world. And that's exactly what they did. Will we do the same? Will we hang with world-changers, or will our friends cause us to live a life full of regrets?

Read Proverbs 13:20. What's the key to becoming smart?

PRO TIP

Albert Pujols
"Following Jesus Is My Main Thing"

With 3,000 hits and 600 homers to his credit, Albert Pujols is only the fourth baseball player to scale those dual peaks. He has earned a place with the major league's best: Willie Mays, Henry Aaron, and Alex Rodriguez.

Yet Pujols remains humble. He says the Lord gave him his talent and ability, but he insists it's not his main job. His job, he says, is to go out and to share what God has done in his life. If he can't play tomorrow, he's going to keep following his main thing.

"My advice for young Christian fans and people who are not saved is if you don't know Christ, get to know Him before it is too late," Pujols says. "For those who know Him, keep our eyes on the Lord because there are so many temptations out there and traps that Satan will set for us. Walking with the Lord and having Him in our hearts—those are the things that are never going to fail."[3]

A tip from Albert Pujols's life: Make following Jesus your main thing.

3

Making Friends—
and Keeping Them

There I was, in a new school in a new town—*alone.*

My friends, my basketball team…everyone and everything familiar to me was 400 miles away in another state. My family and I pulled up our roots in Lincoln, Nebraska, packed all our things into a moving truck, and headed south to start a new life in a new place—Missouri.

I set my tray on an empty cafeteria table and just stared at my lunch. Earlier, when I'd been standing in the food line, a kind elderly lady plopped each item on my plate. "Anything else, dear?" she asked with a big grin. I smiled back (at least for a second) when I noticed a Cardinals hat over her hairnet.

"No, thanks—this is good," I said.

At least my food looked familiar: chicken nuggets, tater tots, and an apple. *But is it as good as what Mrs. Steiber served up back home?*

I was about to find out when a voice interrupted my thoughts.

"Hey, uh…is it okay if I sit here?"

It was another new kid—a boy I'd met that morning when a counselor was showing me around.

"I'm Dillon," he said, sticking out his hand. "I saw you during the tour. I moved here from Kansas."

"I'm Chris," I responded, shaking his hand. "I came here from Nebraska."

"Go, Huskers," he said.

I laughed. "I'm going to miss those games. Memorial Stadium was amazing!"

"We don't have a major football team in St. Louis—at least anymore," Dillon said. "But we do have the Cardinals. And people here are crazy about them."

"I know," I said, laughing. "Did you see the cafeteria lady?"

"Her hat!" he replied, nodding his head. "That's awesome!"

Suddenly, my unfamiliar surroundings weren't all that strange to me. And suddenly, I wasn't feeling so alone. My new friend was changing everything.

I can't think of too many things worse than sitting alone in a crowded cafeteria.

Enter a room filled with faces you don't recognize (especially if you're the new kid at school), and your stomach knots up. Your knees shake, your mouth feels like it's full of peanut butter, and that cool new T-shirt suddenly looks like you've run a marathon in it.

As you look around the room, you notice something strange (definitely a mystery): Everybody is hanging out in herds, or cliques—small, exclusive clumps of guys and girls who share the same interests. Keep looking, and you'll see all kinds of herds: athletes, gamers, surfers, skaters, science buffs, and artists.

You already know friendship is important. But why does it feel so weird to be alone? And just why do guys and girls hang out in herds, anyway? One word: *acceptance*. No one wants to be left out. When a small group of friends takes us in, we don't have to worry about being alone. Are herds bad? Well…yes and no.

Jesus hung out with a herd—those who followed Him. They often met by themselves for prayer, teaching, and good times. But whenever outsiders came along, the group opened up to them. Jesus was not selective of whom He befriended. He accepted everyone.

As we try to make more friends, what can we learn from Jesus? Keep reading.

WINNING WORDS

"You are better off to have a friend than to be all alone, because then you will get more enjoyment out of what you earn. If you fall, your friend can help you up. But if you fall without having a friend nearby, you are really in trouble. If you sleep alone, you won't have anyone to keep you warm on a cold night. Someone might be able to beat up one of you, but not both of you. As the saying goes, 'A rope made from three strands of cord is hard to break'" (Ecclesiastes 4:9-12 CEV).

WINNING TACTICS

- *Start with a smile.* Being friendly is important, and a smile enables you to communicate acceptance without saying a word. Though it seems like kindness doesn't come easy for kids, you'll be surprised at how many friends you can make—and keep—by being understanding. And when you put others at ease with a smile and a little kindness, you'll give them the courage to open up.

- *Risk reaching out.* A kid named Dillon took a risk and sat at my table in the cafeteria. We started talking and really hit it off, and now we're good friends. The truth is, most kids are going through the same kinds of things as you—the same pressures and fears. And we all pretty much want the same thing: friends. So take a risk and say hi.

- *Communicate.* That's how friendship grows. Nothing strengthens a friendship more than two people sharing their thoughts and feelings with each other. Talking and connecting allows us to know and to understand one another. So it's a good idea to watch those put-downs. Say something positive to your friend. Be different and make it a habit to toss out compliments. Joking around is one thing, but constantly hurling insults or laughing at people's mistakes can really hurt. Words can be weapons, but they also can bring healing.

? Read 2 Samuel 9:1-13. When it comes to friendship, are you a promise keeper?

SIX GREAT CONVERSATION STARTERS

- *Sports.* Pretty much a no-brainer, right? Talk about your favorite pro teams, amazing plays, sports you participate in—anything!

- *After-school jobs.* This will reveal a lot about your new friend—and it gives you lots of ground to cover. "It's so cool that you work at a veterinary clinic. Is that what you plan to study in college?" "What's it like making pizzas?" "Do you like working at your dad's store?"

- *Animals.* People love to talk about their four-legged friends. "Do you have a pet?" "What's its name?" "How long have you had it?"

- *Embarrassing moments.* We all love to laugh, and laughing at ourselves can be a great bonding experience. Pull stories from the "I was so embarrassed" files of your life.

- *Faith.* Here's a big part of your life you should share. Talk about what's going on in youth group and camps, and bring up other great things God is doing in your life.

- *Vacations.* There's so much to talk about—traveling, dream vacations, adventure trips…crazy places you've visited. Be creative: "Let's say your parents offered to take you and a friend anywhere you want to go in the world next summer. What kind of vacation would you choose?"

4

When Friends
Do Dumb Things

Sophia stepped through the doors of her favorite sporting goods shop, smiled at the greeter, and then headed straight to the baseball section. The 12-year-old circled a display rack filled with bats and balls, but that wasn't what she wanted. She'd come for a different reason.

Her eyes cautiously surveyed the cashier's station as she pretended to be interested in a water bottle. As usual, the store was buzzing with activity.

Not yet, Sophia told herself. *Too risky.*

She patiently sorted through a rack full of gaudy bobbleheads—all her favorite MLB players. She occasionally stopped and held one up, laughing…just to maintain her act, of course. After what felt like an eternity, Sophia saw her chance. Across the aisle, a man was pointing at a hunting knife, and the cashier was jamming key after key into a lock, trying to figure out which one would open the case.

Now!

Like a wolf attacking its next meal, Sophia swiftly pounced on a leather glove she'd picked out a few days earlier—the $99 Rawlings Elite Series glove her mom said they couldn't afford. *No security tag—good! That means no annoying alarms!*

Without a second thought, Sophia quickly slid the glove into her oversized purse—undetected. And to ensure her cover, Olivia paid for a $9.99 lime-green water bottle. *I needed one anyway.*

"Thanks, miss," the cashier said as she handed Sophia her receipt.

"No, thank *you*," Sophia said with a grin.

Before long, she was out the door and heading through the mall—completely relieved. Just as Sophia dug into her purse and began poking around for enough change to buy a Coke, a sharp voice startled her from behind. "Excuse me, young lady!"

Sophia spun around and locked eyes with a middle-aged housewife. Only this housewife was flashing a badge. "I'm with store security," the lady said bluntly, "and I'll have to ask you to step back inside."

A few minutes later, Sophia's stomach began to churn as she sat in front of a TV monitor, saying everything was a big mistake. Yet right there, before a store clerk, a manager, and the undercover security woman, Sophia could see her criminal act in living color. It was all so vivid. A hidden video camera had caught every one of her clever moves.

"Okay," Sophia said as she pulled the baseball glove from her purse and handed it to the store manager. "I did it—you got your girl. I'm completely guilty."

A tear rolled down her cheek. *Stealing, lying—how could I be so dumb? And what's going to happen now? Will my parents ground me for life?*

My friend Sophia got in a lot of trouble that day. Sadly, though, I know other kids at school who have done even worse things. And here's a little confession: I've made a few dumb choices too—sneaking out with my friends during a sleepover, eating a habanero chili pepper on a dare, letting a friend copy a homework assignment. Not good choices.

So why do smart kids do dumb things sometimes? We'll take a closer look in chapters 17 and 18, but for now let's look at two reasons.

For Sophia, it was a selfish decision—a case of allowing her wants to cloud her thinking. She wanted a fancy baseball glove and wasn't willing to wait. (Sophia also had a problem sorting out right from wrong because she didn't see a problem with stealing.) For me, I wanted to be accepted—and so I ended up learning some hard lessons...more than once, I'm sorry to say.

Here's the thing: If—deep down inside—doing the right thing and pleasing God is really important to us, then we've got to work hard at it. The temptation to steal, cheat, and stretch the truth (or tell only half of it) is always staring us in the face. Unless we consciously decide to make doing the right thing a priority, sin will push us over the line.

Here's another thing: We need to care for our friends, especially when they do dumb things. By helping a friend when they mess up and trying not to make them feel foolish, you may end up with a lifelong friendship.

Know a friend who's slipping? Talk to your parents or youth leader, and get their advice first. Then it's time to reach out. Here's how...

WINNING WORDS

"Brothers and sisters, if someone is caught in a sin, you who live by the Spirit should restore that person gently. But watch yourselves, or you also may be tempted. Carry each other's burdens, and in this way you will fulfill the law of Christ" (Galatians 6:1-2 NIV).

WINNING TACTICS

- *Pray for your friend.* Ask Jesus to show you what to do and what to say. Ask Him to use you as His tool.

- *Go to your friend alone and talk.* See if he will get back together with the right group. Listen to what he has to say, and if he asks for your opinion, be honest and give it. Even if your troubled friend calls you names or laughs at you, keep your friendship open. What your mixed-up pal needs most are *real* friends who really care. If necessary, ask God to help *you* forgive your friend.

- *As you talk, affirm your friend and reject the wrong actions.* Tell her you care about her and that it hurts to see her doing what she's doing. You can say, "It's your choice. If you want to continue doing these crazy things, go ahead. But I think it's stupid!" Let her know you're willing to be her friend no matter what.

? Read Psalm 51. If we sin, what must we do?

Cat Whitehill

Cool Cat Under Pressure

The game rode on Cat's shoulders.

Her team was losing 2–1, and the pressure was mounting. She faked left with her shoulders as she pushed the ball right with the outside of her foot. One second to shoot, and she had an open net. She cranked a shot to tie. Game over!

Cat Whitehill is the most experienced defender on the women's US National Soccer Team. And she knows how to handle pressure on and off the field.

"I always know that God has a plan," Cat says. "I hate to lose. I don't cry much, but I cry when I lose. But I always know that God's going to be there. He has an ultimate plan for me."[4]

A tip from Cat Whitehill's life: Let Christ help you through life's pressures.

5

How to Fix a Broken Friendship

than made the basketball team. *I didn't.* Ethan was invited to a sleepover with guys I used to shoot hoops with after school. *I wasn't.* Ethan got to travel all over the state playing a sport I loved. *I couldn't.*

I felt rejected, and it really hurt.

I tried to keep my cool and not be jealous, but all these things got to me…and I ended up saying some things that I later regretted.

"It's not like it means anything to be on that stupid team," I said to another friend. "They're the worst in the state. I'm better off wrestling."

Ethan heard every word.

Before I knew it, he and I weren't talking or hanging out, and it was starting to make other friendships awkward. At school, we went out of our way to avoid each other—in the halls, in class, in the cafeteria. Our friendship was seriously broken.

Weeks turned into months, but then something completely unexpected happened: We ran into each other after school and were forced to talk.

"So…uh, how's basketball?" I asked.

"Stupid," he said.

My eyes grew big. I couldn't believe what I just heard. "Say what? It's stupid? No way—it can't be. I mean, you made the team…and that's pretty cool."

"No—it's actually really stupid right now," Ethan said. "We're not working together as a team, and the coach is frustrated. How's wrestling?"

I looked him in the eye and smiled. "Really stupid too. Not because of the team, but because of me. I just haven't learned the basics yet, so I'm pretty lousy right now."

We both laughed a little and picked up right where we left off the last time we talked. It felt good to hang out with Ethan again.

"Hey—uh, do you want to come over to my house?" I asked.

Ethan nodded his head. "Yeah. That sounds good."

I really stuck my foot in my mouth and nearly blew an important friendship. The second those ugly words left my mouth and hurt Ethan, I felt foolish—and would have given anything to take them back. Thankfully, I had the chance to make things right. Ethan and I patched things up and fixed our broken friendship.

Careless words, tempers, misunderstandings—lots of things can get us in trouble with our friends. The best thing we can do is take a gutsy step, go to that person, and make things right again. How about you? Do you need to tell someone you're sorry? Do you need to forgive someone who has wronged you?

WINNING WORDS

"If an enemy were insulting me,
    I could endure it;
  if a foe were rising against me,
    I could hide.

But it is you, a man like myself,
> my companion, my close friend,
with whom I once enjoyed sweet fellowship
> at the house of God,
as we walked about
> among the worshipers"
>> (Psalm 55:12-14 NIV).

WINNING TACTICS

- *Say you're sorry.* If you've wronged someone, take responsibility and own up to the mistake. It's hard, but it's the first important step toward mending a broken friendship. "Confess your sins to one another and pray for one another, that you may be healed. The prayer of a righteous person has great power as it is working" (James 5:16 ESV).

- *Ask for forgiveness.* First, tell God you're sorry and ask Him for forgiveness. And then go to your friend and talk things out. "Anyone who hides their sins doesn't succeed. But anyone who admits their sins and gives them up finds mercy" (Proverbs 28:13).

- *Forgive and forget.* If you're the one who has been hurt, take some clues from the Bible: "When you stand praying, if you hold anything against anyone, forgive them, so that your Father in heaven may forgive you your sins" (Mark 11:25 NIV).

? Read Psalm 38:3-4. How does hurting someone affect us?

6

When It's Time to Break a Friendship

Eleven-year-old Jordan and his best friend, Noah, crawled into a car with three older guys. Noah's 17-year-old brother was driving.

Jordan waved to his dad, who was standing on the front porch, and then turned to the driver. "Thanks for dropping us off at the game. My dad will pick us up later, but he wanted me to give you some money for gas."

The driver laughed. "The game? Yeah, right!"

The sarcasm in his voice bothered Jordan—not to mention the two unfamiliar teens crammed into the backseat staring at him. *What's up with Noah and his brother? And since when did they start hanging out together? I thought they hated each other.*

This was the second time this month that the plans had suddenly changed. Driving aimlessly around town, drag racing cars at every stoplight, yelling at pedestrians, and hanging out at a convenience store…this wasn't Jordan's idea of having fun. Besides, Noah's canned lines were becoming vaguely familiar: "If I'd known earlier that the guys had other ideas, I'd have told you. And how was I supposed to know that they were going to pocket some stuff at the store? Listen—nobody forced you to come with us."

Jordan swallowed hard and shook his head, his mind wandering back to his dad's warning: *"Friends can have a big influence on us. Don't let any of them talk you into doing something you'll regret."*

Suddenly, he decided to speak up: "You're right. I don't have to be here. So let me out at the corner—now!"

As he climbed out of the car, Jordan looked at his friend, but Noah just shrugged and slammed the car door. As the car sped down the road, Jordan pulled out his phone.

"Uh...Dad," he said, "can you come pick me up? I'll explain everything when you get here."

The world is filled with lethal people, and some of them are people we know.

I had a friend whose life went down the drain—right into a sewer of bad choices. I could practically smell it every time he came around me. I tried to help him, but then he nearly pulled me into the sewer with him. I felt really sad for him because his life was kind of a mess, but I knew I had to break off our friendship.

Friends who cause us to stumble or stab us in the back when we're not looking aren't friends at all. These are the kinds of lethal people I don't want to hang out with. So what's the right way to end a friendship—and how can we avoid lethal people from the start? I have some ideas...

WINNING WORDS

"Do not be misled: 'Bad company corrupts good character.' Come back to your senses as you ought, and stop sinning; for there are some who are ignorant of God—I say this to your shame" (1 Corinthians 15:33-34 NIV).

WINNING TACTICS

- *When it's time to walk away.* It doesn't take a rocket scientist to know when your friend is making bad choices, yet here's something to think about: When God says one thing in the Bible and your friend says another, it's time to rethink your friendship. For example, we know it's wrong to steal. But if your friend doesn't have a problem with it...well, I think you know what to do.

- *What you should and shouldn't say.* Be honest and point out the thing your friend is doing that you know is wrong (stuff like lying, cheating, stealing, and hurting others). Be clear: "I can't hang out with you if you do these things." Don't be mean by calling him or her names, like liar, cheater, or thief.

- *How to play it safe.* My dad gave me this advice: "Build a set of values right now and think about your actions before you get in a tight spot." So by planning my response and having my beliefs thought out beforehand, I'm more prepared to act as I want to act, not as the group wants me to act.

? Read Proverbs 18:24. What do friends do?

PRO TIP

Ryan Hall
Life on the Run

Ryan Hall loves to run, and he's fast.

In fact, this long-distance runner holds the US record in the half marathon (59:43). That makes him the first American athlete to break the one-hour barrier in the event.

Back in middle school, running set Hall on a faith-building path.

"When God gave me the vision [to run] and I started pursuing that, I lost all of my friends," he says. "It really changed the trajectory of my life, because I was kind of headed down the cool-kid party scene where a lot of kids went on to be party-ers and get into some pretty bad stuff. I remember being like, *All right, I need to make Jesus my best friend* because it was a void I needed to fill. It was at that point my relationship with the Lord really started to grow."[5]

A tip from Ryan Hall's life: Become best friends with Jesus.

7

Are You an Impractical Joker?

I reached down and tied my shoes. The muddy laces were frayed and soggy with long strings hanging off of the ends, and my wet shoes squeaked as I pulled the laces. I didn't really need to retie my shoes, but I wanted to buy some time.

Play it cool, I thought to myself. But I could hear my heart beating in my head. *Why am I so nervous?*

I stood up and took a deep breath. I pushed out my chest and hit it hard with my fist. My friends cheered me on as I climbed onto my bike. *Okay, this is it!*

I had ridden it through the creek, wrecked it on the mud path, and flipped it over several times trying to do tricks. But it was solid, and I knew it could handle the abuse.

I flipped the pedal around backward until it was in the right position. It was crucial that I got a fast start. I squeezed the cracked rubber handles until my knuckles were white. I rocked back and forth as I studied the homemade ramp at the bottom of the hill.

We had spent all day working on that ramp. We borrowed random items from several of our neighbors: a huge rusty barrel, some old two-by-fours, and a partially shredded garden hose. We had big ideas for our bike ramp. Jack wanted to build it so the rider would end up in the creek. Dave wanted to build it on the back road. But Dustin's plan of building it at the bottom of the grassy hill won. And then we spent a lot of time arguing about who would be the brave soul to go for a test run. It ended up being me.

But now that I was standing at the top of the hill, I was regretting my bravery.

I rocked back and forth as my friends shouted out advice.

"Don't forget to lean back when you are in the air," Jack shouted. "Be sure to hit the ramp in the middle," Dustin said. I took a deep breath, slammed my foot against the pedal, and launched down the hill. I pedaled as fast I could—there was no stopping me now.

I didn't take a breath as my feet tried to keep up with the spinning pedals. I had the speed. I was headed straight for the middle of the ramp. And then suddenly it all went wrong.

Out of the corner of my eye, I saw Dave pulling on a long white rope. It didn't make any sense. That rope was tied to the big rusty barrel that was the base of our ramp. As soon as I hit the ramp, the barrel shot forward through the air. The two-by-fours fell apart as they flew in different directions. All the small parts tumbled across the ground. And suddenly, I was flying over the handlebars of my bike. My muddy feet flipped over my head as my body twisted through the air. I let go of the bike as I hit the ground. I couldn't breathe. Every ounce of air had been knocked out of my lungs.

As I opened my eyes, I saw my friends rolling in laughter on the ground. They couldn't even talk because they were laughing so hard. It had all been a joke. The entire thing was just a prank, and I had fallen for it—literally.

I was embarrassed and mad. I wanted to punch them all in the face. *What if I had been really hurt? How could they do this to me?*

I pulled myself up off of the ground, trying to hide my face. I could feel tears forming in my eyes. I wasn't sure if it was because of the pain or because I felt like an idiot. But I knew for sure that I didn't want to be around those guys anymore. I limped over to my bike, set it upright, and started walking home.

"Oh, come on, man. Don't be mad. That was awesome!" they yelled. "Hey, aren't you going to help clean up?" they asked as I walked toward my house.

I love to joke around with my friends, and I've been known to pull a few harmless pranks on people. But what the guys did to me that day really crossed a line. I'm thankful I didn't get hurt— or worse.

The trick to having fun is knowing how to separate what's *harmless* from what *crosses a line.* Have you figured out the difference? My buddies and I learned the hard way, but now we're able to have fun—and live to tell about it.

WINNING WORDS

"How terrible it will be for those
    who plan to harm others!
How terrible for those who make evil plans
    before they even get out of bed!
As soon as daylight comes,
    they carry out their plans" (Micah 2:1).

WINNING TACTICS

- *Ask two questions.* (1) Is this prank harmless? (2) Does it cross a line? A prank is harmless if it's safe (it doesn't cause physical or emotional harm), it doesn't destroy property, and it's something both the "victim" and the pranksters can laugh about later. If your prank doesn't meet these tests, it may be crossing the line.

- *Think about the other person.* Before you set up the practical joke, think about the person you're pulling the joke on. Will he or she be a good sport and take a joke well?

- *Consider the friendship factor.* Always make sure the joke isn't mean spirited and that it won't harm your friendship. Your goal: laughing and having fun.

Read 1 Corinthians 14:33. How does this verse describe God?

8

Your Friends Need a Lifeguard

My dad gripped his bodyboard and waited patiently in the churning surf off Southern California's Huntington Beach. He gazed over his shoulder and squinted—scanning the horizon for the right wave.

Suddenly, he shot into action, beating the water with his arms and kicking to propel himself.

"I got it, I got it!" Dad screamed. "WHAAAAAAHOOO!!"

His timing was perfect—finally! The last few waves had left him tumbling helplessly in the ocean's depths. (Yeah—my dad wasn't a skilled bodyboarder, but he loved the sport anyway.)

He caught the lip of a respectable wave rising beneath him and soon experienced the "slide ride" he'd been seeking. He rocketed atop the curl like a missile homing in on a target, and he rode it to shore.

Several waves later, as the surf began to mellow, he and a friend, Brock, decided to kick back on their bodyboards and soak up the summer sun. Big mistake. They dangled their legs and arms in the warm Pacific water, not even considering the riptides and cross-currents around them.

Soon, my dad and his buddy were floating a billion light-years from reality—lost in crazy conversation and lots of laughs, not even realizing what was happening to them. Next stop: Hawaii!

"Uh—hey, man," my dad said, finally looking toward shore. "I think we're drifting."

"It's your imagination," Brock said with a laugh. "The water is really calm right now. Besides, we can still see our section of the beach."

"No," Dad insisted, "I think we've drifted too far. Look at the people. They're getting smaller. And look at the lifeguards—I think they're trying to get our attention."

Dad and his friend began to paddle with all their strength but seemed to be on a watery treadmill. They didn't move an inch.

"It's like we're trapped in a current," Brock said, gasping for air.

"That's exactly right," Dad shouted. "We're caught in a cross-current. Paddle harder!"

Dad looked up again and spotted the lifeguards swimming toward them.

How humiliating! he told himself. *I practically grew up in the ocean. I just can't be rescued! I'll never live it down.*

Before he had time to think about the consequences, he slid off his board and dug his arms into the water—determined to make it out of this jam on his own. But the harder he swam, the more exhausted he became.

"Come on, man," Brock said as he hopped off his board and began to swim like crazy. "Don't give up. We can make it to shore."

For my dad, every muscle began to cramp. He choked on a mouthful of seawater, went under, and then surfaced again. Suddenly, raw fear surged through his body. "I can't do it," he yelled. "I need help—"

He went under once more, kicked his legs harder, and managed to stick his head above water. He opened his eyes to a now welcome sight: the lifeguard's hand reaching out to him.

With every ounce of strength in him, he flung his arm up and grasped it. "Praise God—I'm saved!"

My dad shared that story as we sat on another beach 3000 miles away—a perfect sandy shoreline near Virginia Beach, Virginia. We were on vacation there, biking, beachcombing, and—yep—bodyboarding.

Dad grew up in California right next to the beach, so he had a healthy respect for the power and danger of the ocean.

"Whether it's the Pacific or the Atlantic, the ocean is deceptive," he told me. "Even when it looks safe, dangerous currents lurk below the surface. And no matter how hard we fight with the water, we just can't make it on our own. We need a lifeguard."

I couldn't help thinking that our faith and our friendships are like that too.

One minute I'm rocketing through life on a smooth course, and then the next, I'm caught in a crosscurrent and pounded by pressure: friends who pull me down, coaches who pile on high expectations, and my own doubts, fears, and stubbornness.

As my dad points out, I have a Lifeguard. Our Lord and Savior Jesus Christ will help me through any problem I'm facing. He'll help me with my friendships too.

Do you trust the Lifeguard? Are you leading your friends to Him?

WINNING WORDS

"Do not fear, for I have redeemed you;
    I have summoned you by name; you are mine.
When you pass through the waters,
    I will be with you;
and when you pass through the rivers,
    they will not sweep over you.
When you walk through the fire,

you will not be burned;
the flames will not set you ablaze.
For I am the LORD your God,
the Holy One of Israel, your Savior"
(Isaiah 43:1-3 NIV).

WINNING TACTICS

- *Ask God for help.* When life gets hard, pray something like this: "Lord, teach me how to trust You more and more every day. Please fill me with Your peace, and assure me that You're protecting me—and that You'll guide me to the right choice. I'm taking Your hand right now, and I'm trusting You. Amen."

- *Trust the Lifeguard.* As we read the Lord's promises in the Bible, we can take Jesus at His word and trust what He tells us. When He says we're forgiven, we can start believing Him. When He says we matter to Him, we can feel more confident about ourselves. When He says He is taking care of us, we can let go of worry.

- *Put away pride.* At first, my dad and his friend were too embarrassed to get help. They wanted to swim out of danger on their own. But the crosscurrents were just too strong. It's that way in life as well. Sometimes we just can't handle a problem on our own. Sometimes we need a helping hand.

? Read Psalm 20. Where must we put our trust?

PRO TIP

C.J. Hobgood
Finding God on the Waves

C.J. Hobgood makes surfing look more like a dance than a sport.

He's mind-boggling to watch! On a long and wedging right-hand wave, the goofy footer throws a big backside air reverse that is literally art in motion. Hobgood is among the world's elite surfers, and his list of accomplishments is impressive—world championship titles and consistently voted among the top ten favorites by fans.

Even more impressive is his faith.

"You'll come to a crossroads in your life where you won't have anywhere else to turn," Hobgood says. "You'll have a decision to make. Everyone goes through it; everyone's human. There will be a time. Give your life to Jesus."[6]

A tip from C.J. Hobgood's life: Following Jesus is the best choice you'll ever make.

9

Be Jesus to
Your Friends

My friend's hands were shaking so violently, I wasn't so sure he could finish the challenge. But I stayed hopeful. I knew the best thing I could do was encourage him.

"You can do this, man," I assured him. "You're roped in, so if you slip, you won't fall. But that's not going to happen. You'll make it to the top."

We were with my parents at a family camp in Colorado. (Mom and Dad were leading it.) I was standing on a narrow wooden platform atop a three-story pole, guiding my friend up. Our challenge: pair up, climb to the platform, stand up...and then take a leap of faith. When we jumped off the pole, we were supposed to grab onto a metal bar that was suspended a few feet away. If all went well and we successfully latched onto it, one of our camp instructors would gently lower us to the ground.

If we missed—well, our challenge would become really intense.

"Keep going," I yelled down to him.

"This is insane, Chris," he said. "Why'd I let you talk me into this?!"

"Because you love me, dude. And you know I have your back."

This time the pole started shaking not because of his nervous hands but because of laughter. My friend was finally motivated and close to joining me on the platform.

Next challenge: getting him to take a leap of faith.

So just where is Jesus in your friendships? Do you take Him to school with you—and to the game? Do others see a reflection of Him in your life? What kind of example do you set?

Whether you realize it or not, your actions are being watched by everybody around you. People hear what you say, and they see what you do, where you go, how you dress, and how you handle victory and defeat. You are Christ's example to others.

Check out Brent's story. This Minnesota kid grew up thinking he was worthless. But then he met a Christian boy who introduced him to Jesus.

> When I was in fifth grade, I detested myself because I was obese. I remember sitting at home one night and taking a wire clothes hanger and beating myself on the thigh until I had big welts. I hated myself.
>
> But then I met a very special Christian friend who showed me that God loves me just the way I am. I desperately wanted to see Jesus in the life of somebody. I liked the way my friend lived out his faith. Through him I met Jesus.
>
> I saw Him through my friend's kind words and big smile. And despite all the bad stuff I'd heard about myself, I slowly learned that I was okay—because Jesus made me. Even "fat slob" *me*!

Ready to "be Jesus" to your friends? Not sure how? Take a look at my ideas. Maybe they'll inspire you to live out your faith on the playing field and in the classroom.

WINNING WORDS

"When anyone lives in Christ, the new creation has come. The old is gone! The new is here! All this is from God. He brought us back to himself through Christ's death on the cross. And he has given us the task of bringing others back to him through Christ. God was bringing the world back to himself through Christ. He did not hold people's sins against them. God has trusted us with the message that people may be brought back to him. So we are Christ's official messengers. It is as if God were making his appeal through us. Here is what Christ wants us to beg you to do. Come back to God!" (2 Corinthians 5:17-20).

WINNING TACTICS

- *Care about others.* Think about all the kids you meet at school and during practice. Does Jesus know each one of them? Does He care about their lives? Of course He does. And He's counting on you to reach out to them, living out your faith and being His witness.

- *Honor God by the way you live.* You'll never bat 1.000, but Jesus will give you the strength and courage to make good choices. Like any good father, He doesn't want us doing things that can harm our souls. But He forgives us when we mess up and guides us (through His Word) on how we should live.

- *Try to be a good friend.* Not a perfect one—just a good one.

Be the kind of guy or girl who doesn't judge or make fun of others, the kind who is loyal and encouraging.

? Read John 15:9-17. What does Jesus want us to do?

10

How to Lead a Friend to Christ

Don't look down! David told himself over and over. *Stay focused on the goal—just as Zach showed me. I won't fall. I can do this.*

The 15-year-old reached above his head and gripped a tiny crevice with his fingertips and slowly made his way up the steep rock face—inch by inch.

This is insane but fun! he told himself as he began to trust the safety harness around his waist.

"Go, Spider-Man!" his buddy hollered down from a ledge 40 feet above, grinning from ear to ear. "You're climbing like a pro."

A pro? Hardly! But the encouragement from Zach felt good. It gave David confidence and kept him going as he attempted his first Colorado climb.

Zach had talked him into it. The two were freshmen at the same Denver high school, and both were really starting to hit it off—which, to David, was nothing short of strange. Zach was "Mr. Extreme": a serious rock climber who hoped to one day lead wilderness expeditions. David, on the other hand, was into art and music.

The two were worlds apart spiritually as well. David was committed to his faith in Jesus. Zach wasn't sure what he believed.

David's mind flashed back to the conversation that had convinced him to spend a day hanging from a remote cliff in the Rockies: "Tell you what," Zach had said to David. "Go climbing with me, and I'll go to church with you. I'll even listen to your endless sermons about this Jesus dude instead of blanking out—which is what I usually do."

David had smiled and stuck out his hand. "Deal."

Now that the big day was here, the artist-turned-climber was starting to enjoy the extreme sport. And before he had realized it, triumph—he joined Zach at the top!

The two fist-bumped each other, and then David soaked in the view. He felt pretty confident standing atop the canyon wall.

Zach glanced at David and blinked. "So I guess it's sermon time," he said, handing David a PowerBar.

"No, I don't have to preach, 'cause you just did!"

Zach shook his head. "Now you're talking nonsense, which is probably a sign of oxygen deprivation or overexposure to the sun or—"

"Don't you see, Zach?" David interrupted. "This whole experience has been a sermon. Rock climbing is all about risk and adventure, which is so much like faith in Christ—and life itself."

Zach folded his arms and wrinkled his forehead. David kept talking.

"Just the thought of climbing this canyon wall made me scared out of my mind. But you showed me what to do, and I listened. It was your voice that got me through the rough moments—and the reminder to 'trust the rope.' It took a lot of faith to do this."

David paused and then pointed to some guys across the canyon who were climbing kamikaze style (solo and without safety harnesses). "Check out those climbers. What do you think of them?"

"They're absolute idiots," Zach snapped.

"What makes you say that?"

"Because kamikaze climbing in this canyon is crazy climbing."

"Why is it so crazy? I've seen lots of people going solo today."

"Oh, please. One wrong move, and you could slip and—" Zach stopped in midsentence and locked gazes with his friend. "Okay, wise guy, I see what you're doing. You're getting me to preach a sermon."

"No sermons," David said with a smile, "just the truth. Jesus really is my safety line in life, my Guide...my Friend."

Zach shook his head again. "Okay—you're actually making sense to me, which means I'll go to church with you. For once, I'm not blanking out."

David nodded his head. "Good. Now, uh, please tell me—how do we get down from here?"

Zach grinned extra big. "Time to trust the rope again!"

My friend David has taught me so much about sharing my faith. It really doesn't have to be hard or scary. Instead, David reached out to Zach with honesty and kindness, and he used something of interest to his friend as he shared the gospel—in this case, rock climbing. Sharing Jesus through our lifestyles really isn't a big mystery. It's something that should come naturally to every believer.

WINNING WORDS

"You are the light of the world. A town built on a hill can't be hidden. Also, people do not light a lamp and put it under a bowl. Instead, they put it on its stand. Then it gives light to everyone in the house. In the same way, let your light shine so others can see it. Then they will see the good things you

do. And they will bring glory to your Father who is in heaven"
(Matthew 5:14-16).

WINNING TACTICS

- *Forget "Christianese."* Just talk—openly, honestly, and naturally. And whether you surf or sing, cook or climb, use your interests to witness for God.

- *Be real.* Even Christians have bad days. We get mad, we cry, and we feel rejected and lonely at times. It's okay to be honest about our feelings with our friends—even people we're witnessing to. The Bible says that God doesn't want us to be fake—in our relationship with Him, in our interactions with others, or in our own lives: "You want complete honesty, so teach me true wisdom" (Psalm 51:6 CEV).

- *Involve your Christian friends.* There's strength in numbers. Besides, getting your friends involved can open the door to greater ministry. You can be like an army that rises up among the extreme sports culture—or among guys and girls on the basketball court, or in the science lab, or...well, you get the picture.

? Read 2 Corinthians 2:15. How does this verse describe our Christian witness?

PRO TIP

Tori Allen
Rockin' It for Christ

Life rocks for world champion climber Tori Allen. Her gift just happens to be scampering up the side of a rock face, but Allen says she has even higher goals.

For example, she tries to encourage people all over the world. At competitions, she throws a stuffed monkey doll to the crowd after a successful climb, just for fun. In her local community, she volunteers to teach others about the beauty of the climbing world, and she speaks out as an advocate for the preservation of outdoor climbing areas. Her tithes have gone to friends in Benin to build a better house for them.

"Every day you wake up, think about the decisions you'll make to change the world," Allen says. "If you want people to get closer to God, then live like that. For me, I strive to always take the high road with decisions. In the short run, it might stink, but in the long run, it may be better. I've always gone above and beyond in everything. 'I can't' isn't in my dictionary. 'If' isn't an option either. It's 'when' I'm going to do things. God gives me discernment to make decisions."[7]

A tip from Tori Allen's life: Change the world for God.

MY ALL-STAR STATS ABOUT FRIENDS

Describe your best friend.

What qualities do you like most?

_____

_____

_____

_____

Tell about a time when a friend had your back.

What happened? How did you feel?

_____

_____

_____

_____

Start a friendship prayer list.

Jot down names of friends you'd like to pray for along with their prayer needs.

_____

_____

_____

_____

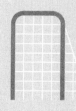

Part 2

Winning with the Team

A Game Plan for Godly Sportsmanship

11

Whose Side Is God On?

A BATTLE FROM THE PAST—
SUPER BOWL XXV

The suspense was agonizing. Jittery fans sat on the edges of their seats while the New York Giants and Buffalo Bills battled for a world championship. It was the final moments of Super Bowl XXV, and the next play determined who took home the Vince Lombardi trophy.

As the kicker lined up his field goal attempt, network TV cameras zeroed in on some unusual sideline activities: About a half dozen Giants players were holding hands, heads bowed, kneeling in prayer. On the other side of the field, some of the Bills were praying too.

Were the teammates praying for some divine direction (the strength to handle Super Bowl stress, maybe?), or were they calling on God to clobber the competition?

Seconds later, it was all over. The Bills' kicker missed a field goal, and the Giants emerged as world champions.

After the game, Giants tight end Mark Bavaro—one of the guys praying his brains out earlier—told a reporter, "Obviously, I was praying for victory."

And Giants coach Bill Parcells said this to a reporter: "I realized a long time ago that God is playing some of these games and He was on our side today."[8]

TWENTY-SEVEN YEARS LATER—
SUPER BOWL LII

It was another Super Bowl thriller with the big win coming down to the final seconds of game play. At first, it looked as if the Patriots had a chance. They were trailing, 38–33, with 2:21 remaining on the clock and a time-out. Not a perfect scenario, but enough time for QB Tom Brady to turn things around.

Brady threw a Hail Mary in the direction of tight end Robert "Gronk" Gronkowski. But then Philadelphia Eagles defensive end Brandon Graham strip-sacked him, forcing him to fumble. The ball rolled off of Gronk's helmet and bounced around for an extra heartbeat, eventually falling to the turf. *Whoa, that was close!*

Rookie linebacker Derek Barnett recovered the ball, allowing the Eagles to run more time off the clock and add a field goal for the 41–33 win.

Philadelphia had its first Super Bowl title!

Moments after emerging victorious at Super Bowl LII, many on the team began praising Jesus Christ for the win. Head coach Doug Pederson was one of them. "I can only give the praise to my Lord and Savior Jesus Christ for giving me this opportunity," he said.

Tight end Zach Ertz, who caught the game-winning touchdown, chimed in: "Glory to God first and foremost." Just days before the game, he told a reporter, "Our number one goal is to make disciples."

And after QB Nick Foles had been named Super Bowl MVP, he couldn't stop thanking his Lord and Savior: "All glory to God."[9]

Through the years, players and fans alike have brought their faith to the Super Bowl stage. But as I watch opposing teams pray for a big win, I can't help wondering something: Does God actually take sides in the game? I mean, could He actually be a Giants fan? Or does He prefer the Eagles…or the Patriots or the Broncos or the Seahawks?

My dad says yes…and no!

Say what?

"Yes, God is a fan of everyone," he told me as we watched the Super Bowl on TV. "That includes every player on the field, every fan in the stands, and everyone watching at home. But no, it doesn't matter to God who wins on the football field…or baseball diamond or basketball court or race track or hockey rink."

Okay, that makes sense. Our heavenly Father loves us all equally—regardless of what uniform we wear. But let's face it: We all want to win, no matter what game we play. And it seems like wherever we turn, someone is competing for something—grades, jobs, money, acceptance, or friendships.

If we let our guard down just once, fumble the ball, lose our footing—*POW!*—it's all over. We're banished to the bench in utter humiliation while the champs strut their stuff down victory lane. Winning feels incredible; losing can ache clear to the bone.

So is that drive to win good or bad? Again, yes…and no! (It's a little of both.)

On one hand, our competitive spirit provides the incentive we need to do better, to sharpen our God-given skill, and to face a challenge. It's a normal drive that the Lord actually put in us.

On the other hand, a competitive spirit can be corrupted by such things as greed, pride, deception…even hate. When we give in to a win-at-all-costs mentality, our sole motivation is to beat the "enemy" rather than to give it our best effort. And that just isn't right. What good is winning the game if, in the process, we're a rotten friend and an inconsistent Christian? I try to direct my own competitive drive toward becoming a better athlete…and a better person. How? Keep reading…

WINNING WORDS

"God will reward each of us for what we have done. He will give eternal life to everyone who has patiently done what is good in the hope of receiving glory, honor, and life that lasts forever. But he will show how angry and furious he can be with every selfish person who rejects the truth and wants to do evil. All who are wicked will be punished with trouble and suffering. It doesn't matter if they are Jews or Gentiles. But all who do right will be rewarded with glory, honor, and peace, whether they are Jews or Gentiles. God doesn't have any favorites!" (Romans 2:6-11 CEV).

WINNING TACTICS

- *Get better game-day goals.* We don't have to turn every game into a contest that proves who is superior. Instead, we should switch our goal from clobbering the competition to making a good shot, executing a good pass, playing by the rules, improving our skills, and setting the right example.

- *Win in life—not just on the playing field.* The Lord isn't impressed with shiny trophies and first-place awards. God looks at other stuff: hearts transformed by His power, eyes focused on His will, and hands involved in His service.

- *Jesus is our biggest fan.* The Lord is right at our side whether we win or lose. And even though we'll compete for just about everything in our lives, there's one thing we'll never have to worry about losing: God's love for us. It's the only thing we can win at no matter what we do.

? Read Proverbs 2:6-8. What things can help us win in life?

A GAME PLAN FOR HEALTHY COMPETITION

- Remember that competition is temporary—as with everything in this world. But God's kingdom lasts forever. Keep your focus on His values and His will for your life.

- Never buy the lie that winners are only those who excel. Our worth as individuals is based on who God says we are—His kids—not on how well we do.

- Be committed to drawing strength from God—especially during competition. Ask Him to change your desires and attitudes. Ask Him to teach you to put the fun back in the game.

- Keep in mind that 1 John 5:11-12 (NIV) is the only yardstick to measure true winners and losers in life: "This is the testimony: God has given us eternal life, and this life is in his Son. Whoever has the Son has life; whoever does not have the Son of God does not have life."

12

Heart of a Champion

It's torture. Gut-wrenching, muscle-depleting, lose-your-lunch torture.

The 800-meter race is only for the strong of heart. The problem is, I'm strong of heart in basketball, lacrosse, football, wrestling—and just about any other sport.

But track?

This is insane! I tell myself. *Running around in circles is not my idea of fun!*

Yet for some crazy reason, my friends talked me into an end-of-the-year competition that brings together all the middle schools in my town. Any student can enter, and the winners get medals, pizza, bragging rights, and a field trip to a nearby amusement park—all expenses paid. No kidding! During the last week of classes (right before summer break) while everyone else is slaving away in stuffy rooms, the champions get to have fun outside.

Food, fresh air...no schoolwork! It doesn't get any better than that, I reasoned. *I'm winning this!*

At first, I thought running would be easy—even fun. *I run a lot in basketball and lacrosse, and I'm in pretty good shape. It's just the practice that'll be lousy.*

Man, was I wrong. Dead wrong.

So here I am, enduring the grueling punishment of what many consider the hardest race. Each lap is like a punch in the gut, and I'm even more convinced of what I knew all along: Track was invented by deranged, Groot-like aliens who gave up guarding the galaxy so they could torture unsuspecting kids!

As I near the finish line, my mind begins to play tricks on me. And suddenly, I can't stop thinking about roller coasters…and greasy pizza. (A very bad combination!) Waves of nausea lap at my tonsils. I imagine myself morphing into a human geyser and erupting like Old Faithful—with bits of breakfast burrito and orange droplets of Gatorade raining down on the crowd!

Push through, I tell myself. *I can do this. I'm going to win!*

As I keep running, my inner-athlete takes over. While I hate practice, I hate losing even more…so, thankfully, adrenalin surges through my body and keeps me going.

Head erect, legs pounding, arms pumping in the sticky May air, I'm securely in the lead through the fourth turn. I'm mentally and physically committed.

And then something amazing happens. The nausea disappears, and I focus on the prize.

Seconds later…I cross the finish line in victory!

My friends cheer as I raise my arms high in the air. A big smile stretches across my face.

I get the bragging rights and a break from schoolwork, I tell myself. *But maybe I'll take a rain check on the pizza!*

The Bible compares our Christian life to a big athletic competition, something like the one I won. (In a second, you're going to read all about it in Philippians 3:12-15.) To run the race, we have to get in shape. We have to be disciplined and focused on winning the prize. It's super important that we develop the character of a champion. It isn't easy, but we have help.

Can you hear God cheering you on?

Is your heart tuned in to His?

WINNING WORDS

"I have not yet reached my goal, and I am not perfect. But Christ has taken hold of me. So I keep on running and struggling to take hold of the prize. My friends, I don't feel that I have already arrived. But I forget what is behind, and I struggle for what is ahead. I run toward the goal, so that I can win the prize of being called to heaven. This is the prize that God offers because of what Christ Jesus has done. All of us who are mature should think in this same way. And if any of you think differently, God will make it clear to you" (Philippians 3:12-15 CEV).

WINNING TACTICS

- *A champion is disciplined.* This is an absolute priority. How many athletes can skip training and still win? Zero. It's the same way with our faith. Without spiritual training—prayer, Bible study, church—we can't grow. Without daily training, we won't develop and mature as believers. Paul (the guy who wrote the verses above as well as a bunch of great books in the Bible) said that a competitor goes into strict training. He beats his body. He strains. Stretches. And presses on. This kind of discipline is not an accident. Paul said, "Train yourself to be godly" (1 Timothy 4:7), and "All who take part in the games train hard" (1 Corinthians 9:25). Discipline puts feet on Christ-followers' faith.

- *A champion is focused.* My dad once asked me, "How do you see your life as a Christian? Are you a competitor or a spectator? A leader or a follower?" In Philippians 3:13 (CEV), Paul said, "I struggle for what is ahead." He didn't look back. He reached forward. He was committed to his faith—to sharing Jesus with his friends and living the Christian life. If we are going to be champion Christians, we must be 100 percent focused on knowing, loving, serving, and growing in God.

- *A champion is committed to godly character.* What is it? The Bible describes it as "Christlikeness." Paul said that his goal and desire were to be more like Christ (Philippians 3:10). Jesus is our leader. Our example. Our "spiritual coach." And He calls on us to follow Him.

Read Revelation 3:16. What kind of characteristic will God "spit out" of His mouth?

PRO TIP

Adrian Gonzalez
Leading His Team to Greatness

First base is an important position on a Major League Baseball team, one filled with pressure and high expectations from team owners. The MLB player who consistently rises to the challenge is New York Mets No. 23—Adrian Gonzalez.

As a five-time all-star, Gonzalez has a .288 average with 311 home runs in 14 major league seasons. He's a confident athlete and a true example for others to follow. Engraved on his bat is "PS 27:1," which reads, "The LORD is my light and my salvation—whom shall I fear? The LORD is the stronghold of my life—of whom shall I be afraid?" (NIV).

"God has put me in a situation where I have a big platform to profess Christ to people, so I've got to take advantage," Gonzalez says. "He's given me abilities to play this game, and I'm grateful for that. I do the best I can with them, and in return, try to be the best disciple I can for him."[10]

A tip from Adrian Gonzalez's life: Share your faith with others.

13

Big-League Attitude

I t was a humid summer day, busy with one of America's favorite pastimes—baseball.

The scorching Florida sun bore down on the players, and waves of heat shimmered across a red clay diamond. At the bottom of the ninth inning, the scoreboard showed two outs. Ron, the pitcher, wiped sweat from his brow, squinted, and sized up the next batter. The pressure was on, and his hands began to tremble. Just one more out and his team would take the championship.

Ron took a deep breath. *I can do this*, he told himself. *Never say can't.*

He wound up and delivered. With a resounding crack, the batter made contact, line driving the ball toward the mound.

Ron lunged for it, scooped up the ball, hurled it to first, and threw the runner out. The crowd leapt to its feet, jumping and cheering for the young athlete. It was a big win from the mound, not to mention an amazing play.

But here was the most incredible part: The pitcher wasn't a pro or even in the minors. He was a 13-year-old who had delivered major-league moves despite having cerebral palsy—a serious disability that often made even walking a chore.

Early in life, Ron decided that he'd never allow life's challenges to get the best of him, and his dad was right by his side, coaching him and helping him to grow a big-league attitude. Whenever Ron began to say "I just can't do it," his father gave him words of encouragement: "Never say 'I can't.' Always say 'I can,' then find another way to accomplish the task. As a man of God, set your standards high, turn to Him for guidance, and take a step of faith!"

Ron looked toward the stands and caught his dad's eyes. A giant grin stretched across his face as his father raised his arms in victory.

"We did it, Dad," Ron whispered. "Never say can't."

Many years later, Ron still follows his dad's advice, and he's even committed to passing it on to other kids. Today, he spends his weekends cheering on Little League players—always echoing those four words that changed his life: "Never say 'I can't.'"

Ron may not play in the pros, but he has a big-league attitude that he caught from his father. "I've always lived for sports, especially baseball," he told my dad and me. "When I was seven, I desperately wanted to play T-ball. So Dad promised to work with me. First, he bought me a right-handed glove, and we tried to play catch. But I couldn't hang on to anything. My right hand just didn't have enough strength to grab the ball. I cried. I was so frustrated. I kept saying, 'I can't.' But my dad sat me down and said, 'Never say "I can't." Always say "I can," then find another way to accomplish the task.'

"Dad bought me a left-handed glove—and it worked. For the first time in my life, I caught a ball. Today, I'm still catching baseballs."

Ron insists that victory on the field and in life can be ours if we exercise our brain cells, not just our muscles. We need to keep our cool under pressure and have a never-give-up attitude. "Maybe this handicap was a blessing in disguise," he says. "It has forced me to never give up on anything I try. I always look for alternative ways of tackling other problems in life. I try never to let a problem get the best of me—just as my dad had said."

I want this kind of attitude too—not just on the field but in life. Ron is one of those guys who inspires me to be a better athlete and a better kid. So here's how I'm growing the right attitude...

WINNING WORDS

"The LORD is a mighty tower where his people can run for safety" (Proverbs 18:10 CEV).

WINNING TACTICS

- *Find strength in God.* The Lord has given us strength to accept life's challenges—even when we think we can't handle them. Pray and ask Him for the confidence to face a challenge.

- *Tell yourself "I can."* We really can accomplish any goal we set our mind on. We can because God made us all smart problem solvers, just like Ron. Even better, the Lord gave us all very special gifts, talents, dreams, and the abilities to go after them.

- *Don't let self-doubt or fear hold you back.* When the pressure is on, sometimes we're our own worst enemies. We are sometimes scared of athletes who seem bigger, stronger, and faster than us. We clam up when we're around kids who seem way smarter than us. But Scripture tells us that we can be confident just the way we are: "You created the deepest parts of my being. You put me together inside my mother's body. How you made me is amazing and wonderful. I praise you for that. What you have done is wonderful. I know that very well" (Psalm 139:13-14).

 Read 1 Chronicles 28:20. Does this verse give you confidence? Why or why not?

14

How to Pray Before and After a Game

Strength, speed, agility, endurance, explosiveness—I felt like my football team had it all. And even better, we were a tight, unified machine on the field, ready for battle...ready to win.

"We're the best," my coach yelled to the team in a loud, sing-song voice. "We can't be beat. We will never accept defeat! Who's the best?"

"WE ARE, COACH!"

"Dedicated, motivated, we will not be underrated. We will have victory! Who will have victory?"

"WE WILL, COACH!"

Tonight was the matchup we'd spent all week preparing for, and our heads were in the game. We'd studied our opponents and learned their strengths and weaknesses. We'd strategized the moves that would give us the edge, and we trained hard: stretching, running, and doing bench presses, depth jumps, vertical jumps, squats, leg presses, dead lifts, shrugs, and rows. My muscles were about to explode, and so was my head. But I knew I had the mental toughness to face the competition.

I looked up from the gridiron and spotted the opposing team, huddled on a corner of the field doing the same thing we were doing—getting hyped for the game.

My gaze took me to the crowded bleachers, where I spotted my parents sitting among dozens of other families. They waved. I gave them a quick thumbs-up. The sidelines were also crowded with the marching band, the cheerleaders, and other parents who'd volunteered to grill bratwurst and serve chips and Cokes to everyone. *This is a really big deal here in Missouri*, I thought to myself.

Suddenly, my concentration was broken by our team captain.

"Time to pray, pastor," he said to me.

"Say what?" I asked. "Pray? Pastor?"

"Yep…I'm talkin' to you. Lead us in prayer, okay?"

"Uh—yeah, sure…I can do that."

That's so cool! I thought to myself. *We have the physical and mental toughness. Now it's time for some spiritual toughness. And the guys on the team call me "pastor" because they know I'm a Christian. And the captain asked me to lead everyone in prayer.*

And then it hit me. *Uh-oh…he asked me to pray out loud with God and everybody listening. YIKES! What am I going to say?*

"So…let's bow our heads and, uh, pray," I said nervously. "Okay, here we go…"

I was both excited and freaked out, which was sort of crazy.

What should have been like breathing—talking to my heavenly Father—suddenly became really scary. *What should I say…and how should I say it? What if I mess up? What will God think?*

Thankfully, my parents are helping me to calm down about prayer. They explained that God loves hearing from us and wants us to pray more about anything and everything—big stuff that shakes our lives as well as in the tiny troubles that annoy us.

"Giant needs are never too great for His power," Mom says. "Small ones are never too small for His love."

Did you know that God not only hears our prayers but also *answers* them and *moves through them*? (Not always in the way we may think though.) Second Chronicles 7:14 says that when we pray, God promises results. Prayer can secure His aid and move His mighty hand.

"'Have faith in God,' Jesus said. 'What I'm about to tell you is true. Suppose someone says to this mountain, "Go and throw yourself into the sea." They must not doubt in their heart. They must believe that what they say will happen. Then it will be done for them'" (Mark 11:22-23).

Prayer is important, so let's learn how to do it.

WINNING WORDS

"This is how you should pray.
'Our Father in heaven,
may your name be honored.
May your kingdom come.
May what you want to happen be done
    on earth as it is done in heaven.
Give us today our daily bread.
And forgive us our sins,
    just as we also have forgiven those who sin against us.
Keep us from sinning when we are tempted.
    Save us from the evil one'"
    (Matthew 6:9-13).

WINNING TACTICS

- *Talk directly to God.* That's our goal with prayer. It doesn't matter to Him whether we stand or sit, fold our hands or extend them toward Him. What matters is that we pray from the heart—with honesty, seriousness, and faith. If you're asked to pray out loud with the team, it's okay to think about a few things to say ahead of time. Just make sure it all expresses what's inside your heart.

- *The Lord helps us pray.* Here's what the Bible says: "In certain ways we are weak, but the Spirit is here to help us. For example, when we don't know what to pray for, the Spirit prays for us in ways that cannot be put into words" (Romans 8:26 CEV).

- *Just have a conversation with Jesus.* Scripture instructs us to do this: "Be anxious for nothing, but in everything by prayer and supplication, with thanksgiving, let your requests be made known to God; and the peace of God, which surpasses all understanding, will guard your hearts and minds through Christ Jesus" (Philippians 4:6-7 NKJV).

Read Matthew 6:5-13. What must we do when we pray?

PRO TIP

Kevin "KJ" Johnson
Handling Life's Ups and Downs

Kevin Johnson (nicknamed KJ) has had 17 broken bones and reconstructive knee surgery, not to mention a couple of concussions. His body has been bruised and beat up—yet that's not stopping him from being a champion motocross racer.

He has snagged gold at the Summer X Games in the Speed and Style event, and he never fails to wow his fans with mind-boggling tricks. Still, KJ wants something even better. He wants his faith to be on display as he opens the throttle. He wants everyone to know the source of what drives him.

"One race, I led the whole race, and then the bike broke the last lap," KJ says. "I just had to pray. My anger turned to peace, and God changed my heart...Prayer has become my ally. I would fall apart without it. I pray after every race, win or lose, because there's so much to be thankful for."[11]

A tip from Kevin "KJ" Johnson's life: Pray always...about everything.

15

What to Do If You Don't Make the Team

Faster. The coach's words screamed through Jason's head. *Faster on each turn. Seventy laps. No rest.*

He and the five other speed skaters looked like a long train as they raced around the 400-meter ice rink. Jason was tailing the lead skater for now, but on the next turn, the leader would pull off and drop to the rear of the pack. Then it would be Jason's turn to pace as hard as he could with the other guys following him.

Every muscle was surging with pain, and his heart was pounding so hard it hurt to breathe. *How'd I ever get nicknamed Flash?*

"GO! GO! GO!" barked the coach as Jason took the lead.

Jason ignored the stinging razors that tore through his quads and focused on his goal—competing in the Winter Olympics.

Building endurance and pushing his body to its limit six to eight hours a day, six days a week, was the only way to get there. "But if I didn't believe it was God's will for my life," he told other racers, "I wouldn't spend another second on the ice."

Was it God's will for Jason to make the US Olympic team?

I asked myself that question when I first heard his story. (Jason is from my hometown, Colorado Springs, but he trained in Milwaukee.)

Jason is committed to his sport, and he's a talented speed skater, so it's hard to imagine him *not* making the team. But still, the competition is tough. A lot of guys try out for a limited number of spaces, so the thought crossed my mind, *What if it just doesn't work out? How will he handle the rejection? I mean, I didn't make my high school basketball team—even after playing the sport my entire young life. That really hurt. But an Olympic dream? How do you get over that?*

I soon got my answer, and it made my heart skip a beat. "No," he told my dad, "I didn't make the team."

The next words out of his mouth blew my mind: "Speed skating in the Olympics has always been my dream, but now I can look forward to whatever else God has planned for me. I know that everything that happens to me has a purpose. God's purpose. And His purpose is always best."

Athletes like Jason have anchored their lives to the right goal— seeking God's will, not just their own dreams. They set goals, plan ahead, train, and set off in one direction, knowing that God may take them down a completely different track. And not only do they discipline their bodies for competition, but they train their spiritual lives too—reading the Bible, praying, and seeking God's guidance. That's why they're not devastated when hard times hit or if they don't get what they'd hoped for. They know that God is for them, and His ways are best.

WINNING WORDS

"Do you not know?
    Have you not heard?
The Lord is the everlasting God,
    the Creator of the ends of the earth.

He will not grow tired or weary,
>   and his understanding no one can fathom.

He gives strength to the weary
>   and increases the power of the weak.

Even youths grow tired and weary,
>   and young men stumble and fall;

but those who hope in the LORD
>   will renew their strength.

They will soar on wings like eagles;
>   they will run and not grow weary,
>   they will walk and not be faint"
>   (Isaiah 40:28-31 NIV).

WINNING TACTICS

- *We can't lose our true identity.* It's okay to identify with a team and with a sport. But if we try to base our total identity on these things, we risk losing it altogether...and becoming very disappointed. Jason had the right perspective: "I can look forward to whatever else God has planned for me. I know that everything that happens to me has a purpose. God's purpose. And His purpose is always best."

- *Get on an eternal track.* Just as an athlete gives his or her all to a sport, Christians need to give the same commitment to God. Once we put God first in our lives and trust Him with our hearts, He will show us His power—power that we never imagined. His will for us is far greater than any of our own dreams and goals.

- *We need to stay balanced.* Our enemy the devil knows exactly the right buttons to push in our lives. He sees our weak points and goes after them. But he can't destroy us.

No matter how bad life gets, no matter how much we mess up, Jesus still loves us. But it hurts the Lord when we disobey Him. Christ weeps for our sins, and He yearns for us to come back to Him. When we blow it, we need to confess our sins to God and ask Him to help us get our lives on the right track again.

Read Romans 8:28-39. How can you be confident that God is for you—even when things aren't going your way?

16

What to Do If Tempers Flare

I t was an intense b-ball clash between two of the town's biggest middle school rivals. And when I say *clash*, I mean that literally.

One second, a player was scrambling for a loose ball against an opponent…and then the next, the two guys started shoving each other. One guy was even pushed into the crowd.

But the scene grew even worse…

Several more players jumped up from the bench and joined the melee. Referees and coaches struggled to pull apart the tangled mass of boys.

Hey, this is basketball, not wrestling. What's going on?

Once everyone calmed down and the players took a knee, the wrath of the coach put some healthy fear into the home team. He took a full minute locking eyes with each player on his team, which must have felt like an eternity. Eventually, the coach spoke—calmly and quietly.

"What happened today will never, ever happen again on my team," he said. "You are not animals; you are athletes. And I expect you to behave like an athlete…with discipline, dignity, teamwork."

The coach made his point very effectively. Some of the guys lowered their heads in shame. Others were crying. *Ouch.*

Regardless of the game, every athlete gets mad at times. I know I have.

It usually happens when I'm not playing my best or when a teammate isn't hustling—and we're losing badly. At other times, an opponent gets in my head, throwing me off my game. That can churn up all kinds of frustration inside. And the coach can push my buttons too...especially if he constantly chews me out.

Anyone with the tiniest competitive bone in his or her body knows that winning rules on the court or the field. So in the heat of competition, tempers sometimes flare. It's what we do with our anger that matters. Do we shove the competition? Do we bad-mouth the coach or scream at a teammate? Do we end up being thrown out of the game?

Guess who gets hurt the most by these angry reactions? Yep— you guessed it: first your team and then you. Losing your cool will cause your performance to drop for three reasons: You'll lose focus on the competition, you'll shift your attention to retaliation instead of making a good play and winning the game, and you'll lose your confidence and will get sloppy.

WINNING WORDS

"My dear friends, you should be quick to listen and slow to speak or to get angry. If you are angry, you cannot do any of the good things that God wants done" (James 1:19-20 CEV).

WINNING TACTICS

- *Know your triggers and redirect the anger.* Identify what pushes your buttons—whether it's trash talk or the ref's poor call—and then try to brush it off. Instead of letting your anger get the best of you and ruining your game, redirect it to game play. Let it give you an extra energy boost so you can run faster and play even harder.

- *Learn how your opponents think.* When you get an elbow to the nose or are knocked down by your opponent, take it in stride. Don't think of it as a personal attack. If you allow your opponent to get under your skin, you'll spend more time being angry and less time enjoying the game.

- *Instead of getting mad, learn...and grow!* If you make a mistake, use the anger or frustration you feel to improve your next play. Don't rehash the past.

? Read Proverbs 29:11. How do wise people behave?

PRO TIP

Kelly Clark
Extreme Sport, Extreme Faith

Kelly Clark is one of the most famous snowboarders in the world. She won Olympic gold in 2002 and bronze in 2010, and she's an X Games champion. But that's not what most people remember when they meet her. Instead, it's the snowboarder's contagious smile and her joyful personality that stand out.

Clark says it's because she loves Jesus. The athlete even had a sticker made for her board that says, "I cannot hide my love for Jesus." That sticker's message is the foundation of her whole life.

Today, Clark is on the prayer team at her church, and she loves telling others about the source of her joy. "God is blessing me so much by not only allowing me to do what I love to do, but by allowing me to tell others about him at the same time," she says. "Everything I do is about Jesus."[12]

A tip from Kelly Clark's life: Be bold and share Christ with others.

17

Why Sane Kids Do Crazy Things

O kay, I was stupid.

I had no experience on a mountain bike, yet stretched out below me was a triple-black-diamond, ride-at-your-own-risk trail.

This is going to be so easy, I thought as I slid on my sunglasses. *After all, I'm riding downhill. How hard can that be?!*

Minutes later, I was rocketing out of control—in hyperdrive. Gravel sprayed in every direction, and squirrels took cover. I blasted around hairpin curves and shot over neck-fracturing obstacles.

Fortunately, I was wearing a helmet, but I didn't have those trendy (but protective) spandex biker shorts—or body armor for that matter. And I'd never been taught the basics, like how to avoid a painful "groinplant" (striking a part of your bike with your groin).

In biker lingo, I was a "geek" (a beginner) being "hammered" (violent body slamming) on a "super gnarly trail" (terrain that's difficult, technical, and steep). I had entered a world dominated by the "incredibly honed" (adept but obnoxiously egotistical riders), and my biker destiny looked grim—serious "leg burn" (to fry one's leg muscles through extreme exertion), followed by a bone-jarring "body dab" and a nasty "face-plant" (unusually gruesome mountain bike mishaps).

Amazingly, I survived my first downhill ride. And when I reached the bottom, my biking partner—a skilled mountain biker who was obsessed with danger—pointed to another trail (disguised as a cliff).

"Now comes the real challenge," he said with a sinister grin. "Next, we head *uphill*!"

My eyes bulged out, and I gasped. And then everything went black!

By now, you've figured out that I'm a sports-crazed kid. I love everything about competition, and I'll try just about any sport at least once. But here's something that's still a mystery to me: Why is it that an otherwise sane kid will do crazy things sometimes? (Me included.) I mean, flying down a steep trail on a mountain bike without any previous experience was…well, pretty crazy.

But at the same time, it was thrilling. The danger got my heart pumping. My blood raced, and my head swam with the rush of adrenalin. It was like sitting through a scary movie or taking a big drop on a roller coaster. I know the car won't jump off the tracks… but what if it did? What if it flew off while I'm going 80 miles an hour? Where would I land? On top of the soda stand, maybe? Would I get a free Coke and a ticket refund?

All I know is, fear can be thrilling. I guess that's why adrenalin-craving kids like us do crazy things—and even take crazy risks. (More on that in the next chapter.) Every day, we experience low levels of "commonsense fear." You know, good, respect-inducing fear—the kind that tells us not to step into the street in front of that oncoming semi…and that we'd better do our homework so we don't fail class and face the wrath of Mom and Dad. Sometimes a little alarm triggers inside our heads, shouting, "Respect the consequences! Stay away from the things that can hurt or kill you!"

So I guess that's the trick. We need to sort out "good crazy" from "bad crazy"…"good fear" from "bad fear." If athletes like us can figure this out, we'll learn how to make good choices on the trail, on the playing field, and with our friends. We'll even be able to have fun and live to tell about our (good) crazy adventures!

WINNING WORDS

"The LORD himself will go ahead of you. He will be with you. He will never leave you. He'll never desert you. So don't be afraid. Don't lose hope" (Deuteronomy 31:8).

WINNING TACTICS

- *Take your fear to God.* The more I grow up—and grow closer to God—the more I find myself in really scary moments (usually at night). And during these times, I've noticed two things going on inside me: I've feared for my life, but I've also felt God's protection. Call me crazy, but I think it's healthy to experience this kind of fear. When we're scared, it's good to call out to the Lord and feel comforted, knowing that we are in the grip of His protection.

- *Listen to your fear alarm.* God wants us to follow His instructions, which can keep us out of harm's way. Where do we find them? In the Bible and through prayer. The Holy Spirit speaks to our hearts, nudging us away from bad choices or actions that could endanger our lives.

- *Let God drive out bad fear.* Let's say we blow it and do

something dumb. What then? God wants us to take
responsibility for our actions by turning to Him in repen-
tance. He will forgive us, drive out the fear that comes from
doubt and shame, and fill us with the courage to face the
consequences…and once again live in step with Him.

Read 1 John 4:18. What drives out fear? Why is this
good news?

18

Right Risks, Wrong Risks

I t was a serious, lung-straining moment!

Mark was pedaling like crazy as he passed a bunch of BMX racers.

The 14-year-old rider cruised neck and neck with his toughest opponent, and then he attempted a "sling-shot pass" on the next turn. (It's a passing maneuver that takes riders to the outside of a turn as they approach a curve.) If his timing wasn't absolutely perfect...*WHAM!* The guy hot on his tail could do a "block pass"— knocking Mark out of action and out of the heat.

The stakes were high, but this Chester Springs, Pennsylvania, kid took the risk.

"Eat my dust, dude!" Mark yelled as he picked up speed. *Just a little closer*, he told himself. *Just a little faster.*

WHOOOOOSH!

Mark rocketed into the lead and approached the final jump. His heart was playin' keyboards with his rib cage, and his helmet felt like a miniature steam room. But hey, Mark wasn't about to let pain choke his chances for another win.

He hit the base of a jump, popped a wheelie and caught some

air, and then forced the front of his bike back down to the ground. (Just for the record, this slick maneuver is called "speed jumping.")

Just before making a bone-jarring landing, Mark extended his legs—using them as long, cushy shock absorbers—and then pedaled down a smooth straightaway to a break-the-tape finish. Another win for Mark and another moment in the spotlight!

Mark will be the first to tell you that BMX racing is a risky sport. It's a head-to-head competition that's fast and dangerous— a little like a horse race mixed with a roller-coaster ride. You have to expect injuries and be okay with that, and you're always at the mercy of other riders. You race at high speeds with no suspensions on your bike, so your body becomes the shock absorber.

In less than four seconds, you and seven other athletes reach 40 mph as you zoom down a three-story hill. And then you face the first jump, which is usually when people get hurt. It isn't unheard of for BMX racers to blow out ankles, tear ligaments, break their arms, or bust their knees.

With this sport, riders hit hard—the dirt can feel like asphalt— so you have to be a little bit crazy to want to get up and do it again.

Still, I'd classify BMX racing as mostly a *right* risk.

If you train hard, improve your skills, and put safety first—as Mark does—you're on solid ground. His sport is about so much more than just pedaling and throwing your bike in the air…and crashing. It's an activity that takes a lot of skill to gain and maintain speed. And BMX racing builds character. It's definitely harder than it looks, and it requires precision maneuvers. Riders must practice daily, stay in shape, and learn to be accurate with their moves.

So what's a wrong risk? It can be doing something that's life-threatening just to feel cool or to impress someone. You know what I'm talking about. Some of your football buddies dare you to smash open a steel door— helmet first. A couple of popular girls convince you to try car surfing (jumping on the hood of a moving car) in the school parking lot.

"Betcha I can."

"Betcha can't!"

"Betcha I can."

SLAM.

My dad tells me that many injuries (even deaths) among kids happen because of senseless dares and accidents—pushing the limit and being reckless while skateboarding, skiing, bicycling, or running across the street. Some guys and girls think they are invincible. They've survived a few risks and think that proves they won't get hurt.

Let's sort out the right ones from the wrong ones...and learn how to take risks for God.

WINNING WORDS

"Have I not commanded you? Be strong and courageous. Do not be afraid; do not be discouraged, for the LORD your God will be with you wherever you go" (Joshua 1:9 NIV).

WINNING TACTICS

- *Take risks for the right reasons.* God is calling us to break out of our safe, comfortable lifestyles and take risks for Him. Here's what the Bible tells us: "Then Jesus spoke to his disciples. He said, 'Whoever wants to be my disciple must say no to themselves. They must pick up their cross and follow me'" (Matthew 16:24).

- *Take an eternal risk—follow Jesus.* Some of life's biggest risks come by doing what the Lord says, even when it doesn't always make sense to us—stuff like turning the other cheek when you'd rather get revenge, standing up for what's right when it would be easier to blend in, and going against what the crowd says is right in order to do what God says is right.

- *Take an eternal risk—serve Jesus.* The thrill is there. The adrenalin flows. Your heart will race. But you'll also hear the God of the universe cheering you on—and that's the biggest thrill of all. What are some things you can do? Jesus gives some great ideas in Matthew 25:31-46. Activities like feeding the hungry, clothing the naked, taking care of the sick, and visiting people in prison. People who need a friend are all around you.

  ? Read Matthew 25:14-30. What does this passage say about risks?

PRO TIP

Tim Tebow

Playing with a Higher Purpose

Ever since he stepped onto a national stage, Tebow-mania has swept the country. Who can forget the images of Tim Tebow kneeling before a football game to pray and then praising God after a game—whether his team won or lost.

Tebow is a multitalented athlete. He's a skilled QB, a Heisman Trophy winner, a first-round NFL draft pick, and the "Mile High Messiah" who led the Broncos to a six-game winning streak. Today, he's a professional baseball outfielder with the New York Mets.

Back in his college football days, he used a white grease pencil to print *PHL* on top of a black strip underneath his right eye and *4:13* under his left eye. The idea was to share Philippians 4:13 (NKJV)—"I can do all things through Christ who strengthens me." It was Tebow's version of three-second evangelism.

Later, he began taking a knee and praying in public.

Tebow explained it this way: "One of the reasons I get on a knee is because that's a form of humbling yourself. I want to humble myself before the Lord and say thank you for this opportunity."[13]

A tip from Tim Tebow's life: Humble yourself and give the glory to God.

19

Soaring over Defeat

Captain Charlie Plum was a legend among US naval pilots—a guy who could hardly be described as a failure. He put his life on the line in Vietnam during countless combat missions, he survived six years of captivity as a prisoner of war, and later in his career, Charlie helped to establish the Navy's elite Top Gun school in Southern California.

Yet it was a brush with defeat as a kid that helped mold him into a national hero.

Growing up in Kansas, Charlie lived for basketball. He imagined one day leaving the cornfields for fame and fortune in the NBA. But there was a tiny hitch in his big plan: He couldn't seem to lead his junior high team to a single win. After what felt like his "millionth loss," Charlie turned to his coach and poured out his heart: "I let you down—again. I guess I'm just a failure."

His stern mentor nodded in agreement and responded, "If that's what you believe, then I guess you are."

Puzzled and a little shocked that his coach didn't offer encouragement during his dark moment, he asked him to explain.

"Son, life is full of choices," the coach said. "If you choose to believe that you're a failure and get stuck in this sort of mindset, then that's probably how you'll turn out. But if you choose to handle adversity with the right attitude—if you strive to grow from failure—then you'll ultimately be a winner."[14]

That advice changed Charlie's life. Though this young man never found stardom in professional sports, he grew up to be a military hero. And the coach's words were put to the ultimate test behind enemy lines.

Captain Charlie Plum is one of my heroes. I want to be like this top gun, never letting defeat take me out. I want to overcome and ultimately be a winner. My dad says the moments in life that truly mold our character are those filled with embarrassing flops and fumbles, not shining triumphs.

So how about you? Are you committed to handling adversity with the right attitude? Are you allowing God to turn a stinging flop into a soaring success?

We can forget our flops and look to the future with hope. Here's how…

WINNING WORDS

"Lord, I have gone to you for safety.
    Let me never be put to shame.
You do what is right, so save me and help me.
    Pay attention to me and save me.
Be my rock of safety
    that I can always go to.
Give the command to save me.
    You are my rock and my fort.

My God, save me from the power of sinners.
Save me from the hands of those who are mean and evil"
(Psalm 71:1-4).

WINNING TACTICS

- *Don't turn your back on God when you fumble.* He's always there—so we need to reach out to Him. Not only will He comfort us and help us through the humiliation of defeat, but He'll actually turn our sorrow into joy.

- *Don't give up because of an embarrassing flop.* The Lord likes to transform flawed kids into heroes who are fit to accomplish His purpose. We should never let life's blunders get in the way. Instead, let God have His way.

- *Don't let defeat bring you down.* It's all about attitude. We can strive to be winners if we maintain positive mindsets and hearts that are faithful to God, regardless of our circumstances.

? Read John 14:22-36. What should we do when we struggle with doubt?

What Coaches Demand

Suzie was late for class—again.

The 13-year-old trembled at the thought of facing another lecture on tardiness. She dreaded the other students even more—their smirks, their rolling eyes, and their piercing jabs.

I hate middle school, she told herself.

The young athlete could still taste the chlorine from the pool as she stood solemnly in the empty school hall, mustering up enough courage to enter her first-period class. Suzie took a deep breath, combed back her wet hair, and gently eased open the door.

It was a typical day for Suzie, an Olympic-bound seventh-grade swimmer from Arlington, Virginia. With her parents' permission, Suzie's coach blocked out her entire day, which began and ended in the pool. She was up at four in the morning for breakfast, in the pool promptly at five for a two-hour morning workout, and at her first-period class by eight—but she rarely made the tardy bell. She studied during lunch, dozed through fifth and sixth periods, and made it back to the pool by five.

"Push yourself, Suzie," her coach would often yell during workouts. "Come on—no pain, no gain. Want to make the Olympics? It's got to hurt. You've got to do better."

Pain, training, more pain, more training. That was Suzie's life. Her entire world centered on swimming, which left her very little time for being with friends and doing all the everyday things most kids did. But in her words, "I'm an Olympian in training. Swimming is my life!"

Her hard work and determination were paying off. Before she had started the eighth grade, she'd been invited to enter a national swimming competition—one more lap toward her Olympic dream.

On the day of the race, her coach's voice echoed through her head: "Push yourself. No pain, no gain. The Olympics are in your future."

The lean swimmer curled her toes over the edge of the starting block and meditated on the serene blue water below her. *I have to win this event,* she told herself. *This will get me to the Olympics. This is why I train so hard.*

Her parents, her coach, the spectators, the cheers of other swimmers in the distance quickly fused into a dreamlike blur as she fought back fear and took the plunge. Her legs kicked, and her arms stroked as hard as they could.

She was swimming with her eye on gold—future Olympic gold.

She was swimming with her heart set on a dream—being an Olympic champion!

Suzie took first place that day, and she immediately thanked her coach. Her dreams are within reach, and it's all because she's tuned in to this very special mentor.

I'm tuned in to my coach as well—actually, all four of them: my football, wrestling, lacrosse, and golf coaches. Each one teaches, inspires, demands, encourages, pushes, and leads. I've seen how they can turn ordinary kids into extraordinary champions.

The Christian journey is a lot like training for competition, isn't it? We identify ourselves with Christ, we practice spiritually, we discipline our hearts and our minds, and we press ahead with our "eyes on the prize"—eternity with God.

At times, the competition is exciting—and at other moments, it's downright exhausting. Life gets turbulent too. When we feel overwhelmed, how can we stay in the competition? By shifting our focus from the challenge we face to the guidance of our Coach, Jesus Christ.

WINNING WORDS

"Losing self-control
leaves you as helpless
as a city without a wall"
(Proverbs 25:28 CEV).

WINNING TACTICS

- *Our coaches demand attention.* They've been watching us closely and see our abilities, which include our strengths and weaknesses. We need to listen to them when they give us direction because they really do know what's best.

- *Our coaches demand commitment.* Sometimes practice overwhelms us and we want to quit. But if we stick with it and finish what we started—lessons our coaches love to teach—we'll discover that we can do way more than we ever thought possible.

- *Our coaches demand trust.* Like me, you're learning two

important things about competition and faith: Living the Christian life is often hard, yet we can make it if we choose to trust the Coach.

 Read Luke 9:23-24. What's the cost of being a Christian?

Jason Stevens
Faith on the Field

PRO TIP

Rugby is a tough sport, and the players tend to be a tough crowd on and off the field. It takes a lot of guts and a lack of fear to slam bodies with guys the size of NFL linebackers—without pads. And that aggressive mentality often drives rugby players into a hard, no-boundaries lifestyle.

Pro forward Jason Stevens knows. Yet this former player for Australia's Cronulla Sharks stood apart from the crowd. He gave his life to Christ and decided to set an example for his teammates.

"Sports is such a great place to build relationships," he says. "It's a great opportunity to show people your faith. My coach told me I'd earned his respect because I trained and played hard, and that gave me a passageway to speak into people's lives and hearts. You have to earn the right to be heard. You can't cut corners—you have to have integrity."[15]

A tip from Jason Stevens's life: Be trustworthy and live with integrity.

MY ALL-STAR STATS ABOUT COMPETITION

Jot some thoughts about your team.

How do you handle the competition? What would make your team stronger?

_____

_____

_____

_____

Describe a victory and a flop.

How did it feel to win? How did you handle defeat?

_____

_____

_____

_____

Share some right risks and wrong risks you've taken.

Based on what you've learned, what's the difference?

_____

_____

_____

_____

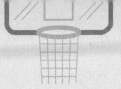

Part 3

Winning with Your Class

A Game Plan for A+ Encounters with Classmates and Teachers

21

When *Cool* Gets Cruel

Toby wasn't like any of my other friends at school.

He wore camouflage hoodies instead of Nike jerseys. He loved hunting and the outdoors, and he was really into classic rock…and country! He spoke with a Southern accent and would say "Yes, sir" or "Yes, ma'am" to adults. He'd hold doors for women and girls, and he loved riding around in his dad's four-wheel-drive Ford pickup, which looked sort of like a monster truck with a huge roll bar behind the cab and mud splattered all over the sides.

I guess Toby was a little too country for the kids I usually hung out with—guys and girls who love sports—and he wasn't very popular. But Toby just didn't care, and that made him cool to me.

He'd talk endlessly about his older brother who was in the army…and how he wanted to enlist when he was old enough. "It's a tough life and a little crazy," he told me as we sat together in the cafeteria. "There was a time when the sergeant major made my brother run until he puked. And then he made him clean the latrine with a toothbrush. *My brother's toothbrush!*"

I couldn't stop laughing even though his story wasn't that funny. I guess it was the way Toby delivered it.

My friends, on the other hand, would mock him.

"I guess you're sitting at the loser's table now," Mason, a guy I usually ate with, told me later.

"No," I replied, "because I wasn't sitting by you!"

"Ohhh," another friend groaned. "Chris punked you, dude." He then gave me a fist bump.

Mason just blinked. "No, really—why are you hanging out with Country Boy?"

"I like him—he's cool," I said.

"Cool?" my friend said. "Are you serious?"

"Completely serious…all the time," I said. I then got up, dropped some garbage in the trash, and headed out the cafeteria doors.

Stay calm and stand your ground, I told myself. *Maybe Toby is on to something. Maybe we just shouldn't care about being cool. I'd rather just be…me!*

So what's with the "cruel cool code"? I don't know about you, but I hate it. Yet wherever I go—school, the mall, church—I notice a lot of kids buying into it.

What's it like where you live?

The next time you walk into the cafeteria, try a little experiment. Look around you. If it's anything like my school, you'll see cliques—herds of guys and girls who never seem to cross an invisible line that separates different groups.

The cool kids claim one part of the room. The preppies, serious kids, skaters, and surfers each hang out in another. The science and computer kids try to lie low somewhere in a corner.

It's not fair, and it doesn't always make sense, but the sad truth is, we've all been sized up, labeled, and forced into a rigid social group.

WINNING WORDS

"My friends, don't be afraid of people. They can kill you, but after that, there is nothing else they can do. God is the one you must fear. Not only can he take your life, but he can throw you into hell. God is certainly the one you should fear! Five sparrows are sold for just two pennies, but God doesn't forget a one of them. Even the hairs on your head are counted. So don't be afraid! You are worth much more than many sparrows" (Luke 12:4-7 CEV).

WINNING TACTICS

- *Don't buy a lie.* It's a lie that measuring up as a kid means living up to an impossible "cool code"—defining yourself by what others think is cool instead of being yourself.

- *Don't play the popularity game.* This is the game of doing what the crowd says is socially acceptable. Though the rules are different in each part of the world, here are a few of the most familiar ones: wearing the right clothes, acting a certain way, and keeping God at just the right distance (at least in public).

- *Don't look to the crowd for acceptance.* If you do, you'll never be satisfied. Instead, be like Toby and my Christian friends who aren't caught up in what others think. Be the person God created you to be—that's the coolest, best person of all!

? Read Hebrews 13:5. What will help us to be content?

22

Cool Redefined

I opened my Bible to have devotions, wanting to learn more about the life of Jesus—and ended up getting a lesson on *cool.* Actually, *cool* was redefined.

In the book of Matthew, Jesus said, "Come with me," and four brothers who fished for a living dropped their nets and followed Him. They left everything behind—their jobs, their houses, and their friends. Here's what happened...

> Walking along the beach of Lake Galilee, Jesus saw two brothers: Simon (later called Peter) and Andrew. They were fishing, throwing their nets into the lake. It was their regular work. Jesus said to them, "Come with me. I'll make a new kind of fisherman out of you. I'll show you how to catch men and women instead of perch and bass." They didn't ask questions, but simply dropped their nets and followed.
>
> A short distance down the beach they came upon another pair of brothers, James and John, Zebedee's sons. These two were sitting in a boat with their father, Zebedee, mending their fishnets. Jesus made the same offer to them, and they were just as quick to follow, abandoning boat and father (Matthew 4:18-22 MSG).

Amazing, isn't it?

There must have been something about the Lord's face—a strength matched with gentleness and something like love that attracted people to Him. When He spoke, His voice must have been compelling. After all, He was God in the flesh!

The four brothers set off on an incredible adventure that became so much more. They had joined a revolution that was going to change history. For the next few years, they watched as Jesus healed the sick, brought people back from the dead, and spent endless hours reaching out to the lost and the lonely—those whom the world would rather have forgotten.

Now that's *cool* redefined!

If there was anyone who really knew Jesus, these men certainly did. They shared a deep and uncommon connection with the Savior. The brothers lived with the Lord 24-7, walking hundreds of miles with Him and never once looking back. And Jesus made them His inner circle, His closest friends—even members of the "big 12" (the original apostles). Their amazing faith helped to turn the world upside down (actually, more like right side up).

Simon, Andrew, James, and John left behind their old life for something—*Someone*—much greater.

Are you ready for something greater too? Are you tired of the rigid cool code? Like me, are you sick of playing the popularity game? Then it's time for a change. It's time to let the One who created you and everything in this world, not the so-called popular people, control your life. It's time to let the God of all eternity, not a passing crowd, define what is and isn't cool. I'm trying to leave behind my old life too, and I'm taking some clues from Jesus. Here's what I'm doing.

WINNING WORDS

"Don't live the way this world lives. Let your way of thinking be completely changed. Then you will be able to test what God wants for you. And you will agree that what he wants is right. His plan is good and pleasing and perfect" (Romans 12:2).

WINNING TACTICS

- *Find your worth in what God thinks of you.* My whole life, I've heard that God loves me. And I know that He allowed His Son, Jesus Christ, to die on a cross and pay the penalty for my sin—and your sin too. So why don't we act as if this is the most incredible news we've ever heard? If God—the One who created us—says we are awesome, why do we follow what other kids think is cool? We can feel good about ourselves just as we are…because that's the way God made us.

- *What the crowd thinks is so important often isn't the most important thing.* Everyone wants a more attractive body and a smarter brain. And most of us would be thrilled to be famous, talented, and wealthy. But the Bible says God wants something that's even more important: "So don't worry. Don't say, 'What will we eat?' Or, 'What will we drink?' Or, 'What will we wear?' People who are ungodly run after all those things. Your Father who is in heaven knows that you need them. But put God's kingdom first. Do what he wants you to do. Then all those things will also be given to you. So don't worry about tomorrow. Tomorrow will worry about itself. Each day has enough trouble of its own" (Matthew 6:31-34).

- *What does God want from us? EVERYTHING!* Especially

things like trust, obedience, and commitment. And the more we get to know Him, the more He helps our confidence to grow and our self-image to improve. We don't need massive muscles or a monster-sized IQ to feel good about ourselves. He accepts us just as we are. "May you have power together with all the Lord's holy people to understand Christ's love. May you know how wide and long and high and deep it is. And may you know his love, even though it can't be known completely. Then you will be filled with everything God has for you" (Ephesians 3:18-19).

? Read Proverbs 29:25. Whom should we trust?

PRO TIP

Kevin Durant
Winning-Shot Maker Wins with Christ

He's at the top of his game.

Kevin Durant's team, the Golden State Warriors, won the NBA finals in five games, and he was named the finals MVP. He even made the game-winning shot in the finals against an NBA legend he'd looked up to since the ninth grade—LeBron James.

The Warriors were trailing the Cleveland Cavaliers with less than a minute to go. In spite of the pressure, Durant hit the shot of his life—a three-pointer. The young star described that as one of the best moments of his life.

But the very best choice, he says, was committing his life to Jesus Christ. "I believe God's love for me, the sacrificial death of Jesus for my sins and His grace, not my good works, are what saves me," Durant says.[16]

A tip from Kevin Durant's life: Trust that Jesus saves.

23

Handling Peer Fear

L ate spring had cruised right into summer, and I suddenly had lots of free time on my hands. As the days grew warmer, I started feeling a little pang inside, a nudge toward a whole new game...something completely unexpected.

"Go on—do it," a friend from school challenged me. "Let's find out if you have the guts to handle it."

It was definitely peer pressure that pushed me into it. That and boredom. But I really wanted to try it—at least once in my life.

So, what am I talking about? The temptation to smoke, drink, or steal?

Nope. I'm referring to a completely different kind of dare, something a whole lot smarter: the nudge to try lacrosse.

That's right—the lax attack! The fastest game on two feet, requiring speed, strength, agility, and serious hand-eye coordination. And it was peer pressure that got me into the sport!

"Betcha can't handle it," my friend taunted me.

"Betcha I can," I insisted.

"Then prove it."

"Okay, I will."

Several weeks later... *WHACK! THUNK! OUCH!*

After joining a local league and training hard, I got to play my first game as a defenseman. Here I was, decked out in some really cool attire—a black-and-silver jersey, a snug helmet, a mouth guard, gloves, shoulder pads, and elbow pads—running up and down a field with a 52-inch stick, body-checking (smacking) my opponents.

I loved it!

My job: Stop the opposing attackmen from creating offense or scoring. Sometimes I had to cover an opposing midfielder.

I quickly learned that in order to succeed at this game, players needed excellent stick skills: scooping ground balls with lightning speed, cradling (running with the ball so it doesn't fall out of the stick's netting), checking (trying to dislodge a ball from an opponent's stick), and shooting.

I'll be honest—I wanted a game where I could legally hit someone. Boxing was out, and I already played football. (I just didn't want to wait until school started again.) As for hockey, forget it. I valued my teeth too much! Lacrosse, on the other hand, was the perfect choice for me.

It was legal to hit someone with a stick if they had the ball, and I could deck them too. (Honestly—look up the rules sometime.)

I had to thank my buddy for the *positive* peer pressure.

"I guess 'Neanderthalball' really is your thing," he joked.

"Actually, it's a civilized sport," I countered. "It's kind of preppy."

"Then we'll have to fix that. How about rugby?"

"You're on!"

I love trying new sports, and I love the (mostly) positive peer pressure I get from my friends—on and off the field. What I don't like is negative pressure.

You know what I mean—the push to do hurtful, harmful, or

sinful things to ourselves or to others...or to take dumb risks. (Remember our discussion in chapters 17 and 18?) Maybe you face the pressure to cheat, lie, pull a dangerous prank on someone, or put something harmful in your body, like drugs.

My dad says handling peer fear begins long before the pressure hits. In other words, wise kids make up their minds ahead of time for how they're going to react to the temptations they'll face. The key is to prepare now for the battles ahead.

I have some ideas.

WINNING WORDS

"No temptation has overtaken you except such as is common to man; but God is faithful, who will not allow you to be tempted beyond what you are able, but with the temptation will also make the way of escape, that you may be able to bear it" (1 Corinthians 10:13 NKJV).

WINNING TACTICS

- *Surround yourself with friends who care about doing the right thing.* I'm talking about trustworthy, like-minded guys and girls—kids who care more about pleasing God and making good choices than about pleasing the crowd. Ecclesiastes 4:12 says single strands of rope are weak on their own, but three woven together will stay tight and strong.

- *See the big picture.* The pressure to fit in with the crowd at any cost may seem unbearable at this stage of your life. But think about this: Will it matter in five years what the popular crowd thinks of you? How about God? Answer: *no* for the crowd but *yes* for God. Check out Philippians 3:12-14. Focus on the finish line, not the stumbling blocks around you.

- *Count the cost.* It's the law of nature: Actions have consequences, which are not always fair. Think about how a choice now might impact your plans, your family, and your future. Here are questions I ask myself: Will a choice I face put me in physical danger? Am I willing to risk ending up with emotional scars? Is momentary acceptance from the crowd worth potentially hurting my future?

Read 1 Corinthians 15:33. What happens if you spend too much time with the wrong crowd?

24

Bullying and Teasing

Bullying is abuse, not child's play, and something *must* change.

My dad speaks around the country and meets a lot of kids who are victims of bullying. Here's what a few of them had to say.

> My teacher says I'm one of the smartest kids at my school, and that makes me feel really good. Even other kids come to me for help when they're stuck on an assignment. But there's this one girl who calls me names and pulls pranks on me. What's worse, one of my so-called friends laughs and joins in on the pranks. I've asked my parents for help, I've talked to my teacher, and I've been praying about it too. But nothing seems to stop the bullying. Please HELP ME!
>
> —*Emma, 10*

> I've been told by my parents and youth leader to pray for a bully. Recently, I gave it a try. During lunch at school, I caught up with this boy who has been teasing me. I sat right across from him and said, "Can I pray for you?" That caused all his friends to laugh, so he got

up, grabbed me by the collar, and started dragging me toward the garbage can. In my head I thought, *I can't let this happen.* So I decked him. That was a bad, bad idea. He came right after me, and I ran, but he caught up and put me in the trash can. Then he punched me and said, "Hit me again and see what happens, you Bible freak!" I was crushed. I tried to do something right, but it went wrong.

—James, 13

I have a *huge* problem with bullies. This one kid constantly picks on me. It feels like torture, and I can't take it anymore. Pleeeeeeease, can someone help me break out of the fear I deal with every day?

—Chad, 12

Several kids from my school have been bullying me online, and it's really hurting my confidence. Why do they hate me so much? I know I'm not very popular or the prettiest girl. I'm a little overweight. But do I really deserve all this teasing?

—Isabella, 11

Sometimes being a kid isn't easy—especially when we have to put up with bullies. Every day, guys and girls everywhere must survive a hostile world that consists of bullies and the bullied, where the strong prey on the weak.

I know kids who feel trapped in a prison of loneliness and shame. They feel terrified too. Some of them try to hide their pain behind emotionless masks, never flinching and always fearing humiliation from their peers. But deep down inside, they're hurting. How about you?

Meet 12-year-old David. This kid is a talented artist who dreams about one day becoming president of his own comic book company—or maybe even filling an upscale New York art gallery with his masterpieces. Yet he feels as if every other kid at his school cares about only one thing—fitting in with the crowd at any cost. Despite being excited about his future and all the possibilities God has set before him, he can't help noticing that too many other guys and girls his age put on cynical acts, making everyone think that nothing but the moment really matters.

"Here's the crazy thing," David says. "I catch myself wondering if something is wrong with me. Some guys call me 'geek' or 'church boy.' It really hurts. Why do kids have to be so cruel?"

Maybe you're a victim. Or maybe you think you have to hurt others in order to avoid being a target. Regardless, like so many other kids, you probably think the only answer is to shut up and fit in at any cost rather than to care or to understand. But as I said earlier, something must change. Here's what I recommend you do…

WINNING WORDS

"You have heard that it was said, 'Love your neighbor. (Leviticus 19:18) Hate your enemy.' But here is what I tell you. Love your enemies. Pray for those who hurt you. Then you will be children of your Father who is in heaven. He causes his sun to shine on evil people and good people. He sends rain on those who do right and those who don't. If you love those who love you, what reward will you get? Even the tax collectors do that. If you greet only your own people, what more are you doing than others? Even people who are ungodly do that. So be perfect, just as your Father in heaven is perfect" (Matthew 5:43-48).

WINNING TACTICS

- *Talk it out.* It's hard, and it can be a little embarrassing, but you've got to tell your parents or a trusted adult what's going on. Don't ever keep it in; that's not fair to you. And if you know of someone who is being bullied, go to a teacher or the principal. It's not snitching; it's helping a classmate. It also shows real courage.

- *Avoid danger.* Proverbs 22:3 says that a prudent man sees danger and takes refuge. In contrast, the simple keep going and suffer for it. This translates into common sense. But what if a bully is strutting in your direction? This leads to the next step. Proverbs 15:1 says a gentle answer turns away wrath. The other half of that verse points out that a harsh word stirs up anger. So here's what you should do: Make every effort to defuse a situation. How? With a direct, calm answer: "Look, I don't have a problem with you. I'm going now."

- *Walk away.* Romans 12:17-18 (NIV) says, "Do not repay anyone evil for evil. Be careful to do what is right in the eyes of everyone. If it is possible, as far as it depends on you, live at peace with everyone." Walking away—instead of standing there arguing at the top of your lungs—is the best way to maintain peace.

? Read Leviticus 19:18. Why do you suppose this verse instructs us to not get even?

PRO TIP

Ed Carpenter
Fast and Furious Faith

Ed Carpenter has a serious need for speed. In fact, he drives a car that sits inches off the ground, has no roof, and goes more than 220 mph.

Carpenter races the No. 20 car in the Indy Racing League's IndyCar Series, and he's fast! He admits the speed is the fun part and the whole reason he competes— he loves the rush of passing cars and winning races.

"All things in life are dangerous," Carpenter says. "I think there is just as much danger driving on the interstate in my street car. I'm a firm believer that when it's your time, it's your time. When you are in a relationship with Christ, you are ready to go at any time. God has a plan for all of us. So the danger doesn't worry me."[17]

A tip from Ed Carpenter's life: Find peace in a relationship with Jesus.

25

Good Kids, Bad Choices?

So do you want the concert ticket or what?" my friend Eddie asked me.

I put down my phone, which I'd been using to look at my *Sports Illustrated* app, and sat up in my seat. It was free time in study hall, so the guys and I were just hanging out. "Well...who'd you say's performing?"

Another friend, Josh, suddenly perked up and joined the conversation. "It's only the concert of the century—the most amazing rock experience everyone's talking about," he said, handing me his phone. "It's Rebel Tonic Toads in their 'Annihilate Your World' tour."

I slipped on the headphones, cranked up the volume, and listened to the first song.

"Oh," I said with a grimace, tapping the stop button. "I know these guys. They're the ones who prance around stage in their boxers, sacrificing live goldfish."

"It only happened once," Lance said defensively. "They're really not that bad."

"Not that bad?" I gaped. "Then what do they mean by 'Rat-tat-tat / Never hesitate to put a cop on his back / Annihilate 'em all / Annihilate your world'?"

"Look, it's just music," Eddie said. "You're the only guy I know who sounds like my parents. Why do you make such a big deal out of stuff that doesn't matter?"

"Yeah...don't be so uptight," Lance added. "It's not like this stuff is going to turn you into a killer or something. This is classic rock, and every guy at church youth group listens to them. What's your problem?"

Uptight? My problem? I sound like...parents? I panicked inside, my internal geek alert blaring in my brain. *I'm not making a big deal out of nothing. But what should I say to these guys—and what should I do?*

I'll admit it: I made up the name "Rebel Tonic Toads." And I don't think there's ever been an "Annihilate Your World" tour...or a rock star sacrificing live goldfish. I'm just joking around about those things.

But I have had conversations like this, and as hard as it is to confess, I've been accused of sounding uptight when I challenge my friends.

Making the right choice is important, so I'm trying to use my critical-thinking skills. In other words, I'm doing my best to question a decision—sorting out the truth from the lies as well as right choices from wrong ones. I'm not perfect at this, but I'm learning, and I'm getting better at it. Here's what my dad is teaching me: "Learn to discern. Use your brain and think through a choice *before* you take action."

God doesn't want us to shut off our brains when we hang out with our friends or when we step through the doors of our schools. And the truth is, kids our age don't always have the best answers. So I'm trying to weigh everything first.

Yeah—it's not always easy putting my faith first, but I know it's the right thing to do. If you're struggling too, try this...

WINNING WORDS

"My child, remember
my teachings and instructions
and obey them completely.
They will help you live
a long and prosperous life.
Let love and loyalty
always show like a necklace,
and write them in your mind.
God and people will like you
and consider you a success.
With all your heart
you must trust the LORD
and not your own judgment.
Always let him lead you,
and he will clear the road
for you to follow"
(Proverbs 3:1-6 CEV).

WINNING TACTICS

- *Don't buy a lie.* Check out Colossians 2:8 (NIV): "See to it that no one takes you captive through hollow and deceptive philosophy, which depends on human tradition and the elemental spiritual forces of this world rather than on Christ."

- *Pray often—pray hard!* The best piece of advice I have received from my parents is actually pretty simple: PRAY!

They encourage me to pray about everything. I can talk to God about my confusion, my fears, and my desire to know the truth. Ask for help. Ask for guidance. Ask for a true heart. Even when you're not sure what you believe, pray.

- *Measure everything against the Bible.* In spite of some people's doubts, God's Word *is* timeless and absolutely, positively accurate in everything He knew was important for us to know. There is room for debate on secondary issues (such as when the rapture will occur), but there are no discrepancies in God's promises, commands, and warnings.

? Read Isaiah 30:21. What will the Word show us?

ASK SOME HARD QUESTIONS

Use Philippians 4:8 (NIV) as a guide to what's entering your eyes and ears: "Finally, brothers and sisters, whatever is true, whatever is noble, whatever is right, whatever is pure, whatever is lovely, whatever is admirable—if anything is excellent or praiseworthy—think about such things."

- Is it true? Does this computer game mock what God says is good?

- Is it noble? Does this movie help me to develop a proper mindset?

- Is it right? Is this TV program causing me to compromise biblical truths?

- Is it pure? Does this concert offer more trash than treasure—is it worth my time and money?

- Is it lovely? Would I be embarrassed if my youth leader found out I read this magazine?

- Is it admirable? Does this song offer wisdom or benefit me in any way?

- Is it excellent? Is this the best possible way for me to spend my time?

- Is it praiseworthy? Am I drawn closer to God because of it?

26

Confidence Clues

"I'M THE UGLY ONE"

Eleven-year-old Logan had a medium build and average looks. But his older sister teased him by calling him ugly.

"Hi, ugly. Wanna go get a burger with me?"

"Hey, ugly! Where's the remote?"

This went on for years. And even though Logan knew his sister loved him, he never felt very attractive—until a teacher set him straight.

"I'm creating a school flier to hand out at the next parent-teacher conference and would love to put your handsome face on the cover," Mrs. Sanders told him. "Would you be my model?"

A stunned expression washed over Logan's face. "Me? I'm not handsome—and I'm definitely no model."

"Child, what on earth are you telling me?" she replied, pinching one of his cheeks. "You have a handsome smile. Will you do it?"

Logan nodded yes…still feeling a little stunned.

"I'M JUST 'LITTLE DUMMY'"

"And the science fair winner is…" Mr. Larson paused. The teacher slowly pulled a card out of an envelope, smiled, and looked up. "Before I make the announcement…"

Several students groaned. "Come on, Mr. Larson—please tell who won!"

"Patience. First, I need a drumroll."

Several students immediately began tapping on their desks.

The teacher scanned his classroom and then locked eyes with 12-year-old Emily. "That's right—it's you, Emily!"

The girl's mouth dropped open. *How can this be?* she wondered. *I'm not smart. I'm just "Little Dummy."*

Emily lived with that nickname practically her whole life. Other kids started calling her that when she was just six because she struggled with saying the letter *R* correctly. Even though Emily was no dummy, she grew up feeling inferior to other kids.

"You're our winner," Mr. Larson assured her. "You're the best scientist in the school!"

"I'M PROVING THEM WRONG"

With a spotter at my side, I gripped the barbell and pushed with every ounce of strength in me. It was six in the morning, and I was training before school with my football team. My buddies and I had been hitting the weights every morning for the past three months, and our commitment was finally paying off. But when I first started, I was new to the team and new to the sport, so I had some catching up to do. Some of the guys poked fun at me, saying I didn't have what it takes.

Instead of getting upset, I used their jabs as a motivation to prove them wrong. *Not tough enough, not strong enough*, I fumed as I attacked the bench press. *I'll show them.*

For three months now, I'd been taking out my frustration on the weights. (That too was paying off.) Today I was benching 115 pounds and had reached my fourteenth rep.

"Come on, Chris! Go for it," my friend Braden said to me. "One more, and you've hit a new record."

"AAARRRGGG!" I groaned as I eked out the final rep.

"That's a new record!" Braden screamed. "You did it! You've lifted the most weight yet...along with the most repetitions!"

I'd been pushing myself, and I was getting stronger. Whenever I looked in a mirror, I could see the difference too. My body was changing, and my muscles were getting bigger. Mostly, I was becoming a better football player. My confidence was growing too.

"Well done," the coach told me, slapping me on the back.

I decided right then and there that I wouldn't be defined by someone else's false labels. I'd prove them wrong, and I'd go on being exactly who I should be—myself!

You and I are on a journey. We're traveling from childhood to adulthood, and our whole world is changing. I'm a little farther down the road, but you're catching up fast.

If you're like me, all these changes you're experiencing and the pressure you face can be hard to handle. Every day, you and I deal with things like peer pressure, school pressure, bullying and teasing—stuff that causes our confidence to really take a beating.

Sometimes people stick labels on us that aren't accurate or fair: ugly, dumb, weak, lazy, clumsy, spoiled, crybaby...you get the picture. And sometimes we feel uncomfortable with all these changes, especially the way we look and feel.

How about you? Are you struggling with confidence?

Hopefully, your parents and teachers have been really good at affirming you, even bragging on you a bit, just as they have with kids like Logan, Emily, and me. When you get those compliments, hold on to them. Remind yourself that you really are okay and that you can do and become anything you want. Nothing is out of reach for you. Remember Stephen Curry's favorite verse that I shared at the beginning of the book? It's a good one to think about when you need an extra boost of confidence: "I can do all things through Christ who strengthens me" (Philippians 4:13 NKJV).

I have some other clues that can help. Take a look.

WINNING WORDS

"'I know the plans I have for you,' declares the LORD, 'plans to prosper you and not to harm you, plans to give you hope and a future. Then you will call on me and come and pray to me, and I will listen to you. You will seek me and find me when you seek me with all your heart'" (Jeremiah 29:11-13 NIV).

WINNING TACTICS

- *Fix what you can fix; accept what you can't.* That's what my dad always tells me. He encourages me to make the most out of what I have, improving the things that are within my power to change and accepting what I cannot change. Dad reminds me that God never tells us, "This is who you are—and who you'll always be." Instead, He says, "Just imagine what you can become." (Check out Zephaniah 3:17 for a really good confidence builder.)

- *Boost your skills; boost your confidence.* Put your energy into a talent or ability that will help you feel good about yourself. For example, if you're a talented musician, artist, or athlete, improve these skills and become the best you can be.

- *Remind yourself that you're normal.* Your world probably feels as if it's full of extremes: extreme energy, extreme emotions, and extreme changes. Yep—like I said, everything *is* changing, and that's all good and all part of God's plan. But in spite of all the changes—and regardless of all the different body shapes and sizes you see at school or in the locker room—you can rest assured that you're normal. You were created exactly the way God designed you to be! You were made by the one and only God Almighty, the God of the universe, and He never makes mistakes. When He created you, He created a masterpiece!

? Read Proverbs 3:5-6. Why is it a good idea to trust God and not our own understanding?

PRO TIP

Elijah Moore
"Jesus Is My Greatest Passion"

Your jaw drops as pro skater Elijah Moore catches big air down a flight of steps and flawlessly reconnects with his board.

Next, he roars past you, making his board dance with some fancy footwork. First, he pulls off the pop shove it, followed by the frontside halfcab kickflip (a few respectable skateboarding tricks). Then he launches into some serious lip tricks and grinds that separate the men from the boys: the backside boneless flip, the frontside board slide, and the nollie backside flip.

Just when you think your eyes are going to pop right out of your head, Moore does something even more courageous: He steps up to a mic and begins to share his faith in Jesus Christ. "I love this sport, but it's not what I'm about," Moore says to a crowd that has gathered at a mobile skate park. "Knowing, serving, and living for Jesus is my greatest passion."[18]

A tip from Elijah Moore's life: Find your identity in Jesus.

27

Wanted: Leaders

Jesus's words in the Bible seemed to jump right off the page as I read them: "Here is my command. Love one another, just as I have loved you. No one has greater love than the one who gives their life for their friends. You are my friends if you do what I command" (John 15:12-14).

I love my family, and I want to give my life to them—serving them and caring for them, I thought as I tried to figure out what Jesus was telling me. *Is the Lord asking me to do this for my friends at school? That's not so easy.*

Some of the kids I knew weren't very kind and lovable.

I thought about all the different cliques, or social groups. Kids seemed to hide in them. And some of the groups were mean to those who didn't fit in. (Remember the invisible line we talked about in chapter 21?) Some of these guys and girls only looked out for themselves and stepped on whoever they wanted in order to climb the popularity ladder.

How does God want me to handle kids like that? And what if they decide I don't fit in? Life would become really miserable.

On the other end of the social spectrum, there were kids who didn't get noticed much. They were sometimes picked on, but mostly they just tried to stay invisible.

I know God wants me to be kind to this group—but how can I help? It's complicated.

Suddenly I couldn't stop thinking about another group—a small handful of kids who didn't really care about the cliques. They seemed real and confident...and showed kindness to everyone. Some were Christians, but not all of them. The thing that set them apart was leadership.

That's it, God, I prayed. *Help me to be like those kids.*

So I made an effort to reach out to every person I met, whether it was the guy on worship team or the girl at school who tried to be invisible. I did my best to see people the way God sees them. I remember saying to myself, *I'm deciding right now that I don't care if I'm popular, and I don't even care if I get picked on for doing these things.*

I decided I wasn't about to hurt people just to fit in. My dad really encouraged me too. Just about every morning before I left for school, he'd pray a blessing on my life: "Lord God, please bless Christopher today. Protect him and give him the courage to be a leader and not a follower. Help him to make a difference in someone's life."

So what happened? Did I receive kindness back as I tried to be kind to others? Not always. Some kids were still pretty mean, and others poked fun at me. But just being nice so others will return it isn't the point. I wanted to serve God and do what was right. I wanted to be a leader.

I learned that when you stand up for what you believe, sometimes just with your life and not even with words, most people will respect you. Some might not agree, but they'll respect you for having confidence, not to mention a backbone. They'll notice that there's something bigger in your life that you live for. Kids our age—and the whole world for that matter—need leaders.

Here's what you can do…

WINNING WORDS

"Don't let anyone make fun of you, just because you are young. Set an example for other followers by what you say and do, as well as by your love, faith, and purity" (1 Timothy 4:12 CEV).

WINNING TACTICS

- *Set a good example*—for your team, for your class, and for your church. Don't just go along with the crowd. Stand up and stand out.

- *Persevere under pressure.* My dad says the best leaders learn to handle pressure as calmly as they handle smooth moments. And if the pressure gets the best of you and you fail, don't get stuck on disappointment. Move forward when the other team wins or someone else is elected class president.

- *Learn the art of negotiation.* Every good leader knows the art of compromise. When we face a choice, sometimes we need to make an offer and even counter that offer with other choices. In other words, don't just accept what's presented to you. Weigh your options and come up with better solutions.

? Read Philippians 2:3. Based on this verse, what's an important leadership quality?

28

Success in School

Abigail was the best soccer player at school—and one of the smartest students.

On the first day of school, one of her teachers handed out the reading assignments, the research paper expectations, the quiz dates, the unit exam schedule—all the stuff that usually made Abigail's stomach hurt.

The 12-year-old was tempted to take the Bart Simpson approach and hide the schedule deep in her backpack, never to be seen again. After all, it made her queasy to think about all this work, and besides, she knew the teacher would remind her as things were coming up…and that would give her just enough time to cram enough facts into her head to get by.

But Abigail decided to give up the Bart Simpson strategy and actually start doing the work. Later, she was glad she did.

None of the students knew that their teacher had a secret hobby as a motorcycle rider. He crashed his Harley into a tree one evening, fracturing some very important body parts. The next day, a substitute teacher arrived in class, found the lesson plan, and carried on.

The weeks streamed by, the teacher continued to mend at home, and the substitute continued to carry out his plans. On the day before the semester-long research report was due, the substitute issued a friendly reminder: "Oh, and by the way, I'm sure you all remember the five-page research project is due tomorrow—along with note cards, bibliography, and…well, everything! Have a nice night!"

While other students began to groan, Abigail let out a sigh of relief. She was ready!

Right after her teacher had handed out the first flood of papers, Abigail had gone through them, put the significant dates on a big calendar, and actually started working on some of the long-range projects. Her research paper was practically finished. All she had left were the final revisions, and her bibliography was ready to type up.

Abigail had taken the steps to succeed. The other students would have an evening filled with stress and panic, but she was going to sleep well!

Bart Simpson is the ultimate underachiever. He's content with average performance, his mind is focused on instant gratification, he doesn't count the cost of his actions, and he wastes energy concocting elaborate schemes for dodging responsibilities.

And when it comes to goals, his head is definitely in the clouds: "I'd like to be the first human to skateboard on Mars. Cowabunga, dude!"

Unmotivated. Unfocused. Unrealistic. But unfortunately, Bart's world describes too many kids…sometimes me included.

Jason, a guy at my church, struggles too. Jason flunked out of school on more than one occasion, and he even got into some trouble with the law.

During summer camp, a counselor asked Jason, "What do you hope to accomplish during your lifetime?"

"I want to be a marine biologist," he responded, "or maybe a photographer."

"Great!" the leader said. "Now how do you think you can achieve these goals?"

"Humph!" Jason grunted as he shrugged his shoulders and poked a stick in the campfire. "I don't do too well at school, and I don't own a camera. I don't know. But each summer my mom takes me to Florida. I think snapping pictures or working with sea animals would be cool."

Who knows—maybe locked inside Jason is a great scientist or a talented photographer. The problem is that he's too much like Bart Simpson—always dreaming but never doing.

I'm trying to be more like Abigail. I want to succeed in school. Here are some clues I'm taking from her.

WINNING WORDS

"Jabez was more respected than his brothers. His mother had named him Jabez. She had said, 'I was in a lot of pain when he was born.' Jabez cried out to the God of Israel. He said, 'I wish you would bless me. I wish you would give me more territory. Let your power protect me. Keep me from harm. Then I won't have any pain.' God gave him what he asked for" (1 Chronicles 4:9-10).

WINNING TACTICS

- *Plan ahead.* It's not unlike Bart or Jason to squander the evening watching the game on TV at the expense of tomorrow's big exam. You don't have to be a straight-A student to figure it out: Blowing off homework assignments and study time will result in more than just bad grades—it can also set bad habits in motion. Abigail played it smart by managing her time well. What's her secret? Three simple steps: She prioritizes her assignments based on due dates, she makes a list of what to do, and she follows her list, marking things off when she's finished.

- *Stay focused.* While you're in class, stop thinking about friends or the game. Listen carefully when the teacher is talking and take notes like crazy. The more you're able to concentrate during class, the more you'll learn—and the less you'll have to study at home. But once you're home, focus on one thing at a time. Projects are more manage-able if you tackle them one by one.

- *Get help.* If you're stuck, there's no shame in asking for help. At home, talk to your parents or your brother or sis-ter, or call up a friend. At school, ask questions if you don't understand something, and don't feel bashful about get-ting help. Flunk failure by going to the one who is teaching you and saying, "I don't get this, and I'm stuck. Would you please coach me through it?" You'll walk away a winner—I guarantee it!

? Read Proverbs 16:3. In order to succeed, what must we do with our work?

PRO TIP

Drew Brees
God Is the Source of His Strength

You step through the gates of the Superdome in New Orleans and suddenly feel overwhelmed. The place is massive. Everywhere you look, you see black and gold, and you hear the roar of tens of thousands of fans cheering. (It holds 76,468 people, to be exact!)

The Saints take the field, and the roar grows even louder. *Really? How's that possible?*

No. 9, Drew Brees, raises his arm in the air and then drops it to his side. That signals the famous chant: "Who dat? Who dat? Who dat say dey gonna beat dem Saints?"

But before the action gets underway, you notice Brees and some teammates doing something really cool: They're praying! Brees became a Christ-follower at age 17 and often tells fans and players alike that God is the source of his strength.

A tip from Drew Brees's life: Turn to God in prayer.

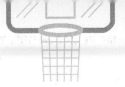

29

Relating to Teachers

I slumped back on the mat, questioning if I was cut out for the sport.

Wrestling was way harder than football and basketball, and I was beginning to see that everything about the sport was tough—the fundamentals, making a pin, and especially the practices. Every day after school (for two grueling hours), Coach Davis put us through a killer strength-training regimen, and then he drilled us on wrestling basics.

"Great job, Chris! You're really improving out there."

I looked up. It was my coach. *Was he serious? Didn't he notice that I lost?*

"Uh, thanks," I said. "But after three months, you'd think I'd actually start winning a few matches. I was even on top in the referee's position. But the kid pulled a reversal…and then he pinned me."

Coach Davis nodded in agreement. "I saw what happened," he said. "And it doesn't feel good to lose. Believe me, I know. I lost countless matches before I started winning. At first, I was terrible… and I was ready to quit. And then things started to click."

Countless losses? Quitting? I thought. I'd never heard him talk this way before.

Coach continued. "In this sport, success comes when you grasp the fundamentals. Learn the basics—like how to do a takedown or an escape—and then practice, practice, practice."

I sat up and shook my head. "I'm trying…but it just isn't working."

He put his hand on my shoulder and looked me in the eye. "Actually, it *is* working. I see so much improvement in you. Don't give up. Persevere, okay? You're learning. Honestly, Chris—you and I are a lot alike."

I sat on the mat in awe. That was one of the greatest compliments I had ever received!

Coach Davis gave me much more than a pep talk that day. He showed me how teachers' brains work and how their hearts tick. He made me realize that teachers are human—not out-of-touch scholars, weird aliens, or heartless robots. They actually feel what we feel, which is why there are three things we should never do if we want to get along with them…

- Don't make fun of them.

- Don't talk back in class.

- Respect their authority.

The truth is, we'll get along with some of them and not so much with others. That's how it is in life, right? But just as it is with parents now and bosses in the future, our teachers have been put in authority over us, so we need to show them some respect.

WINNING WORDS

"All of you must obey those who rule over you. There are no
authorities except the ones God has chosen. Those who
now rule have been chosen by God. So whoever opposes
the authorities opposes leaders whom God has appointed.
Those who do that will be judged. If you do what is right,
you won't need to be afraid of your rulers. But watch out if
you do what is wrong! You don't want to be afraid of those
in authority, do you? Then do what is right, and you will be
praised" (Romans 13:1-3).

WINNING TACTICS

- *When teachers open their mouths to teach, close yours
  and pay attention.* Being disruptive and doing stuff to make
  your friends laugh is never smart. It will only get you in trouble…and on your teacher's bad side.

- *When it's time to talk, raise your hand and participate.*
  Falling asleep in class is a bad idea too. Contribute to
  discussions.

- *When you're not in class, pray for your teacher.* Just like
  other people who can make a difference in your life, teachers deserve your prayers.

? Read Hebrews 13:17. Why is it important to obey our
leaders?

30

Defeating the Homework Monster

Weird organ music filled the room. Lightning flashed. My teacher, Dr. Jekyll, broke into hysterical laughter, "HA, HA, HA, HA…HA, HA, HA, HA!"

Suddenly, he started acting more like crazy Mr. Hyde. He pulled out his red marker, spun around to the whiteboard, and scribbled three spine-tingling words: EXAM NEXT FRIDAY!

"Nooooooo!" I blurted. "Not another test!"

"YES—a test!" Dr. Jekyll laughed. He hunched sinisterly over my desk, wringing his hands. "And it will cover the first thousand chapters—along with my lectures on the rare snails of Kilimanjaro."

A dozen mouths dropped open. I flopped back in my chair and wobbled to the floor. Everything faded to black…

…And then I woke up—drenched in sweat, my covers in a twisted mass.

I started having this recurring dream at the end of summer, and it continued all the way through Christmas break. Yep—I was anxious. Homework assignments were stacking up, term papers weren't coming together, and the constant quizzes and exams gave me migraines. *UGH!* I hated taking tests.

With another school year in full swing, I was definitely falling prey to a familiar routine: panic, worry, and sweat it out. I'd crawl out of bed in the morning, hoping a 7.0 quake would level the school just before my exam. *Hmm…imagine if my football team prepared that way.*

And speaking of football, my coach expected me to practice until five every day, which really cut into my free time. What about my friends? There was very little time for them.

While the pressure was mounting, help and hope came from the most unexpected place: *my teacher.* That's right! And to be honest, she really didn't transform from Dr. Jekyll to Mr. Hyde. Actually, my teacher was really nice.

"No need to stress, Chris," she'd tell me. "Let me help you."

Whenever she'd explain a problem and walk me through the solution—and all the other things that caused me to be stuck— I'd finally get it.

I also got help from the ultimate Teacher. I've learned to give each assignment to Jesus and to ask Him to guide me. God can help us understand a math assignment or send someone to explain it to us. He can even show us how to beat boredom as we slave over each chapter in our history book. And before I take a test, I try to pray. The Lord can calm our nerves and help us to do our best. It really helps knowing that God is nearby: "The LORD will keep you from all harm—he will watch over your life; the LORD will watch over your coming and going both now and forevermore" (Psalm 121:7-8 NIV).

But in order to have a truly stress-free school year, there was one last thing that I needed to do: Defeat the homework monster. Three simple steps took the bite out of the beast.

WINNING WORDS

"Whatever you do, work at it with all your heart, as working for the Lord, not for human masters, since you know that you will receive an inheritance from the Lord as a reward. It is the Lord Christ you are serving" (Colossians 3:23-24 NIV).

WINNING TACTICS

- *Don't procrastinate.* If our teacher assigns us five pages to read each night for a week, we shouldn't put it off. We'll save a lot of pain later if we actually tackle it in small chunks each night just as the teacher assigned it. But if we procrastinate and try to cram at the last minute, the assignment will feel like the dreaded homework monster. It could ruin our weekend and risk harming our grades.

- *Finish your homework.* And actually hand it in. I'm embarrassed to say that I've made the mistake of (a) blowing off a homework assignment altogether and (b) forgetting to hand it in after staying up late to finish it. Both mistakes hurt my grades. A smart thing to do is get organized with a daily planner. Writing down all our upcoming assignments—along with due dates—can help us stay on track.

- *Study in a distraction-free zone.* We need to establish a place at home that can help us to be really productive. Best spots: places away from the TV and video games. Whether it's in a corner of the family room or desks in our bedrooms, it must be a comfortable place where we'll want to spend time.

? Read Matthew 7:7. What does Jesus promise us?

PRO TIP

Simone Biles

God Gets the Glory

Simone Biles won five medals, four of them gold, at the 2016 Olympic Games in Rio. She is the most decorated American gymnast and a four-time all-around gymnastics world champion—impressive accomplishments.

Yet Biles says she couldn't do it on her own. God gets the glory.

"I think God gives every individual something special and mine was talent," she says. "So I never take it for granted. My dad always told me not to waste God's gift that He gave you....I was taught that you can go to Him for anything and He's the One that directs your life."[19]

A tip from Simone Biles's life: Use your talent for God.

MY ALL-STAR STATS ABOUT SCHOOL

Describe your classmates and your teachers.

What do you like? What would you like to change?

_____

_____

_____

_____

Write about the "cruel cool code" at your school.

What types of cliques do you notice? Where do you fit in?

_____

_____

_____

_____

Describe your favorite teacher.

What makes this person so special?

_____

_____

_____

_____

Part 4

Winning
with Family

A Game Plan for Scoring BIG
with Parents and Siblings

Twists and Turns
of Family Life

"Rough water ahead—paddle left!" Jonathan's dad, Jeffery, shouted to him.

"No, Dad," Jonathan insisted. "Let's go left, so paddle right."

"Son, listen to me," Jeffery said sternly. "There are big rocks and strong rapids on the left. We need to veer right. Quickly!"

Jonathan pointed downstream. "But do you see that?" he asked. "There's junk in the water. Maybe it's a fallen tree or something."

"We'll take our chances," his dad responded, digging his paddle and stroking harder. "We'll flip if we hit the rapids."

"But Dad—"

"Don't argue with me. Paddle left. *Now!*"

Suddenly—THUMP! BUMP! The canoe struck a mound of twisted branches clogging a narrow strip of Colorado's Gunnison River. The vessel began to rock violently, but it didn't tip over. Seconds later, the water was calm again.

Jonathan turned around and grinned at his father. "Okay, you were right—this time!"

Jeffery high-fived his son, then slumped back in the canoe.

"I think we're getting the hang of this adventure thing," he said. "Now if we could just figure out…well, *life!*"

My friend Jonathan; his dad, Jeffery; and a dozen other families faced the rapids head-on—and came away stronger. They joined my parents on a four-day canoe adventure through Colorado's canyon country. During the summer months, Mom and Dad often take families on wilderness excursions in the Rockies, teaching life-changing lessons that are best learned with the great outdoors as a backdrop. (And of course, I get to join them.)

Our mission that week: Bust the barriers between kids and their parents.

It takes cooperation and communication to keep a canoe stable, making these the perfect vessels for bringing families together for shared adventure and deepened relationships. But the most powerful moments happened back on shore. Each evening, the kids and their parents gathered around a campfire to "pull off their masks" and talk honestly about the lessons they learned on the river.

"I'm so proud of you, Jonathan, for trusting me today," Jeffery told his son one night. "We were a solid team, which is how God wants us to be."

Jonathan smiled and put his arm around his father. "My heart was racing, and I felt so scared when I saw the rapids," he said. "But you stayed calm. That really helped. And when we came through okay, it gave me more confidence."

The 11-year-old paused, thought carefully about his words, and then continued. "I wish it could be this way at home. It's, like, there's so much stress. Your job, Mom saying we have more bills than money, pressure at school, the way we fight sometimes… Maybe we can start handling troubles like we did today."

Moments like this make me excited. I'm committed to the greatest team of all—my family. Here's what I'm doing to help us win in life.

WINNING WORDS

"Children, obey your parents as believers in the Lord. Obey them because it's the right thing to do. Scripture says, 'Honor your father and mother.' That is the first command-ment that has a promise. 'Then things will go well with you. You will live a long time on the earth' (Deuteronomy 5:16)" (Ephesians 6:1-3).

WINNING TACTICS

- *I'm learning to honor my parents.* God has given them a really big job: providing for me, protecting me, teaching me, and eventually launching me into adulthood. That's a lot of pressure! Like it or not, they aren't just my personal chefs and chauffeurs! Mom and Dad oversee my life, so I need to do what the Bible instructs me and *every* kid to do: "Chil-dren, obey your parents as believers in the Lord."

- *I'm learning to share what's inside.* Opening up more and talking—actually using complete sentences instead of "Nah," "Nothing," and "I don't know"—can help improve life with my family.

- *I'm learning to care more about my family's needs.* Even though we annoy each other sometimes, I love my fam-ily. (Every kid does, right?) But as I move through the teen years to adulthood, I'm cluing in that I can be pretty self-ish at times, acting as if the world revolves around me. I'm

trying to change that. God wants us to put our families'
needs first. How can we make life better for our families?
How can we bring a smile to our parents' faces? Reach out,
help out, care for one another…do kind stuff without being
asked.

Read Proverbs 6:20. What does this verse instruct all
kids to do?

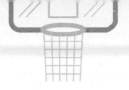

32

Unplugging the Nightly "Clash Royale"

I flopped onto my bed and began to throw a Nerf ball against my Colorado Rockies poster.

"No-o-o-o-o," I mumbled in my best prison warden voice. "'You *can't* have that, you *can't* go there, you *can't* hang out with those friends, you *can't* quit what you started!' When will they learn I'm *not* a little kid anymore? I can make my own decisions."

I was mad. My parents and I had just had another "clash royale"—this time about quitting the wrestling team. There was only a month left in the season, but I was miserable. I hadn't won a single match, and practice was a killer. And I wanted to spend more time just hanging out with my friends—not in a gym, training for competition.

I replayed the argument in my head...

"I'm into football and basketball and even golf," I pointed out. "But wrestling?! It isn't the sport I thought it would be. And we spend way too much time practicing."

"Practice is making you stronger—a better athlete," my dad said. "It's actually going to help you with other sports."

My mom chimed in. "And you're so close to the end. It's hard right now, but you can stick with it for another month. You have to finish what you started."

That's what really pushed my buttons. "No, I can't!" I insisted. "You just don't understand how hard the practices are. I really hate this sport, and I don't even like my teammates. Look, just for once, I'd like to have it my way. If I want to quit, then that's what I should be able to do. It really should be *my* choice!"

But of course, it wasn't. My parents got their way, as usual. That made me even more upset.

At the dinner table, I barely said two sentences—one of which was "Pass the potatoes…please." Later, after my homework was completed, I didn't watch TV with the family. Instead, I shut my bedroom door and lost myself in my music collection.

Meanwhile, I couldn't help wondering a few things. *Why do we go through this every time I say the word* no *or tell them I want my way?*

Mom and Dad were beginning to feel more like prison wardens than parents. I wanted to go back to how it used to be—which was so much easier and a lot more fun. But now…well, life felt so complicated. *Why does it seem like we argue more and more the older I get?*

How is it possible to love a houseful of people so much but to get so mad at them sometimes? How can you live under the same roof with your mom, dad, brother, and sister—be so close to them, know all of their strange quirks—yet feel as if they're the biggest strangers you've ever met? There's only one group that can bring out all these confusing feelings—our family.

My dad explained it to me this way: "Sometimes an 'emotional war' erupts between kids and their parents, and the older you get, the more intense it may feel. But don't panic, because it's perfectly normal. Nearly every child and parent experiences this phase that psychologists describe as the 'war of independence.'"

In other words, with each step we take toward becoming

grown-ups, we become more and more independent of our parents. That's what causes the constant "clash royale." But along the way, there's a lot we can do to reduce the battles and make things better at home.

WINNING WORDS

"Always be humble and gentle. Patiently put up with each other and love each other. Try your best to let God's Spirit keep your hearts united. Do this by living at peace" (Ephesians 4:2-3 CEV).

WINNING TACTICS

- *If you act more grown up, you just might be treated like one.* When Mom and Dad see us throw tantrums and act childish one day and then act mature the next, it confuses them. Our actions speak louder than our size on how ready we are for more freedom.

- *Communicate—even if you don't feel like it.* I admit, this is a tough one for me. Usually when I'm mad, I just don't want to talk. But if we communicate, letting it all out instead of bottling things up inside, life improves...and the clashes become less and less frequent.

- *Show them the* R *word: RESPECT.* They've been our parents for as long as we've been alive, and they've sacrificed a lot to raise us. They deserve it, and the Bible says we need to give it to them: "Honor your father and mother. Then you will live a long time in the land the LORD your God is giving you" (Exodus 20:12).

? Read Philippians 2:14. Why do you think this is good advice for kids?

PRO TIP

Tobin Heath
Thankful for God and Family

Pro soccer player Tobin Heath has a lot to be thankful for.

She grew up in a Christian home and in an awesome family. And everyone in her family was really passionate about Jesus. Even better, she had a great childhood.

But just like so many other kids, by about middle school, the "war of independence" hit, and Heath wanted to start doing her own thing. It wasn't until around the end of high school and the beginning of college that she started to develop her own faith. She says she stopped piggybacking off of her family's faith and started figuring out what it was all about.

Heath knows that everyone has a purpose. For her, that purpose in life right now is soccer. She loves spending time with her teammates in environments where they see how she lives. But in the world of sports, as in everyday life, players go through different ups and downs. You might be on top of the world, or you could be sidelined with an injury. Your teammates see you through the good and the bad. They see where your foundation lies in those moments. Heath has decided to be there for them and to share the love of Christ with them through those times when they're in need and desperate for some truth in their lives.[20]

A tip from Tobin Heath's life: Live your faith among your teammates.

33

Why Parents Sometimes Bug You

Two skis, 3,668 vertical feet of Colorado snow—and my dad at my side, desperately trying to teach me a new sport. That's all some kids need for a wild slide down the slopes. But for me, they were the ingredients for mogul madness!

"I wrestle, and I play lacrosse and golf in the spring and summer," I told Dad as we made our way to a ski lift at Steamboat Ski Resort in the Rockies. "In the fall, I play football. Put me on a field with 11 angry defenders chasing me, and I know what to do. But this? Look...you ski, I don't. This is crazy!"

Suddenly, I stopped in my tracks and took a long, hard look at the 10,568-foot Mount Werner that rose above me. I tore off my sunglasses and glared at my father. "You honestly think I can ski down that—and live?"

My dad patted me on my back. "Come on, Chris," he fired back. "It's a piece of cake—not like we're jumping off a cliff. I want you to experience my sport. We'll stick to the trails for beginners. And after a few lessons from me, you'll love this more than football!"

Just then a snowmobile zoomed past us, hauling an injured skier off the mountain. I pushed my glasses back on. "This is a very bad idea."

I spend a lot of time with Mom and Dad in the outdoors—white water rafting, mountain biking, backpacking, and camping. We have a lot of fun doing these things together. But skiing? That's one of Dad's sports, not mine—which brings up something I've caught myself wondering...and I bet you have too: *We love our parents and usually enjoy spending time with them, but why do they sometimes bug us?*

Skiing with Dad answered that question.

If the "war of independence" hasn't started yet, it will soon. Remember our definition in the last chapter? It's that constant, tension-filled struggle you experience as you move toward the teen years...and on toward becoming your own person.

My moment on the mountain got me thinking about all this. It also gave me some ideas about what I can say to my parents. I really want to stop feeling bugged and start getting back to enjoying our time together. So I've shared three messages with them. Believe it or not, saying these things has really helped our relationship get better. Maybe it's something you can try.

WINNING WORDS

"Be patient when you are being corrected! This is how God treats his children. Don't all parents correct their children? God corrects all of his children, and if he doesn't correct you, then you don't really belong to him. Our earthly fathers correct us, and we still respect them. Isn't it even better to be given true life by letting our spiritual Father correct us?" (Hebrews 12:7-9 CEV).

WINNING TACTICS

- *"Please understand something—I'm not you."* We have a lot in common with our parents (and our siblings), but sometimes our tastes are very different. We often enjoy different things. Maybe your parents are engineers, while you're an artist. Maybe they like reading a novel, while you prefer seeing a novel on the big screen. Let them know you like different things than they do.

- *"Let's learn to trust each other."* Most kids get upset when their parents start acting suspicious for no reason, thinking that their kids are getting into trouble when in reality they're not. We want our parents to trust that we're good kids— even if we stumble. But we've got to remember that trust is fragile and is sometimes hard to build, yet it's universally important to every kid. Talk this out with your parents.

- *"Stay close, but let me breathe."* It hurts when Mom and Dad don't have time for me. But it's just as frustrating when they smother me. So here's what I've told my parents: "Give me some breathing room. Let me try stuff on my own, and even allow me to fail. I'll survive. I might even come out stronger than before. But at the same time, stay close— especially when I fail."

? Read Psalm 141:3. Why is it important to communicate carefully and clearly?

34

What to Do
When You Get Mad

My eyes were set, my chin was protruding, my arms were flailing, and my voice was 20 decibels too loud. But it was my words that probably hurt the most.

"You don't understand. You don't *ever* understand."

With that final angry outburst, I stormed upstairs, leaving my dad standing in the living room, feeling just as frustrated. Oh, I'd be back, and there would be another "conversation"…and yet another explosion. That had been the routine for the past week.

It all centered on my grades…and football practice.

I fell behind with my homework in a couple of classes, which triggered some stern emails. My teachers told my coach, who then told my parents…who ultimately confronted me. So what did my parents do? They pulled the plug on football until I completed all the missing assignments and improved my grades. That, of course, really set me off.

"The coach is holding your spot," Dad had told me earlier. "So you're not off the team. You just have to get caught up. The coach understands, and so do we. I know you don't think we do, but we really get it. Being on the team is important. But schoolwork has to come first."

As I sat in my room fuming, I really couldn't blame any of them, especially Dad. It just felt embarrassing taking a break from the team—the other guys would notice. And I was mad at myself for falling behind. I could handle both. I had just made a mistake, and everything started piling up. It all made me so angry, but I didn't mean to take it out on my family.

I've got to fix this, I told myself.

Once I'd cooled off, I took a deep breath and headed back downstairs.

"Dad, I'm sorry I yelled," I told him. "I'm ready to talk."

Things were really tense there for a while, but amazingly, it all worked out. I patched things up with my family, finished my homework (which instantly improved my grades), and stayed on good terms with my coach. I ended up taking a short break from football, but as it turned out, I wasn't the only one. A few of the other guys had fallen behind too.

It was a hard lesson to learn, but the biggest thing I figured out had nothing to do with football or school. Through it all, I learned the right way to handle anger. I discovered that the Bible doesn't tell us to never be angry or to hide our feelings. Actually, just the opposite. Scripture gives us guidelines on getting angry the *right* way. (Take a look at the verses below.)

The Bible also showed me that if our anger turns into a fight with our family or with a friend, our goal should never be about winning, getting revenge, or trying to even the score. "My dear friends, don't try to get even. Leave room for God to show his anger. It is written, 'I am the God who judges people. I will pay them back,' (Deuteronomy 32:35) says the Lord" (Romans 12:19).

And once we're mad, we need to work toward correcting a

problem, finding solutions, and regaining the peace. "Do not be overcome by evil, but overcome evil with good" (Romans 12:21 NIV).

Here's how we should handle anger and fight…the right way.

WINNING WORDS

"Be angry and do not sin. Don't let the sun go down on your anger, and don't give the devil an opportunity" (Ephesians 4:26-27 CSB).

WINNING TACTICS

- *Be angry without sinning.* While most kids know how to get angry, it's this second step we need to work on. We can actually express our anger the right ways. In other words, the silent treatment and screaming matches don't accomplish anything. If something is important enough to get mad about, then it's important enough to try to work through. Here's what we need to do: (1) Shift our focus away from the emotion and concentrate on dealing with the situation. (2) Step back and pray before we blow up. (3) Channel our anger into action—such as finding a workable solution instead of letting angry words or actions grow into a monstrous blob.

- *Never let the sun go down on anger.* It's important to quickly settle whatever has made us angry. We really can't go to bed until the issue is settled.

- *Uncover what's really bugging you.* Once we calm down, we're better able to get to the source of our anger. In my case, I was embarrassed about taking a break from the team. I thought I would look bad and let down the team.

But once I talked it out with my parents, my coach, and my teachers, I learned that I wasn't alone—and we were about to find a solution. The keys were listening to each other, hearing each other, and finding some common ground. (You'll learn how to do this in chapter 39.)

? Read Matthew 5:24-25. How should we settle matters (and why is this important)?

PRO TIP

Kendrick Farris
Strongman Shares His Secret: Faith

Olympic weight lifter Kendrick Farris knows a thing or two about power—and how to maximize it. But for this athlete, it isn't developed while training in the gym, lifting in a competition, or getting a pep talk from a coach.

Farris says real power comes from God.

He was raised in a Christian home but didn't tap into God's power until he became a young man. "From about the age of 16 to 22 is when I struggled the most," he says. "I've truly humbled myself over the past couple of years, and I've learned about the power we have as believers. Jesus said we would do greater works and I believe that. I don't get bent out of shape about everything that happens in life. I understand that there is a season and a time for everything."[21]

A tip from Kendrick Farris's life: Find power in Jesus Christ.

35

Cool Stuff to Do with Your Brother and Sister

BOWLING ALLEY BATTLE

Chuck eyed the pins, took a step, and released the ball. *THUNK, THUNK...CLUNK!*

"Ouch—gutter ball," jabbed his brother Jeremy. "But you looked good out there anyway. Now watch how the game is really played."

Jeremy fired his weapon down the lane. *SMACK!* Unfortunately, he clipped the edge with his ball, and only three pins tumbled over.

Chuck's other sibling, Justin, nearly spit out a big gulp of Coke as he laughed. "Smooth, Jeremy," he said. "That's exactly how I want to play when I grow up!"

But after Justin released the ball, only one pin went down.

Chuck shook his head. "Face it—we suck at this."

"But the shoes are cool," Jeremy said. "And it beats sitting at home playing that bowling video game Mom and Dad bought us."

Chuck agreed. "Maybe I can break my record. Maybe I can catch up with Justin and hit at least one pin!"

MINI-GOLF WARS

Micah, who had just tied a Hawaiian lei around his head (for "sun protection," he claimed), gripped his putter like a pro and stroked the ball—hard. The ball bounced past a palm tree and a miniature castle—and then stopped just inches from the hole.

Leanor, his sister, burst into laughter. "I don't know what looked more pathetic—your sun protection or your form!"

Micah folded his arms. "Hey, can you do better?"

Leanor lightly tapped the ball, knocking it into the hole. "That's right—that's how it's done," she taunted her brother. "I am a winner. You are a—" She formed the letter *L* with her thumb and index finger and held it up to her forehead.

Micah pulled off his Hawaiian lei and threw it at his sister.

Bowling and mini golfing aren't exactly high-action sports, but they're fast, easy to pick up, and filled with laughs…and they're great boredom-busters during the summer. And if you're lousy at these activities, who cares? Here's an idea: Stop the sibling slug-fests, call a truce, and go bowling or golfing—or try one of a zillion other pastimes—and have some fun together.

I'm an only child, so my slug-fests happen with my friends. But Mom and Dad have lots of siblings, which means our house is always filled with uncles, aunts, cousins, and extended family. Here are two things I hear them talk a lot about…along with their advice:

Sometimes older siblings grow distant. As that happens, remind yourself that older brothers and sisters need a little space and privacy. Honor that, but keep the connection open without smothering them. Ask your older sibling for advice from time to time.

Sometimes younger siblings get clingy. Remember that they look up to you, so spend time with them, even if you're not into the same things anymore. Share advice with them and try to include them in your life as much as you can.

With my parents' help, I came up with some other cool stuff you can do.

WINNING WORDS

"Suppose someone claims to love God but hates a brother or sister. Then they are a liar. They don't love their brother or sister, whom they have seen. So they can't love God, whom they haven't seen. Here is the command God has given us. Anyone who loves God must also love their brother and sister" (1 John 4:20-21).

WINNING TACTICS

- *Share some crazy (kid-only) moments.* Check out my A-to-Z list of favorite boredom busters at the end of this chapter.

- *Laugh with them, not at them.* Having a brother or sister is something to be thankful for, even if they drive you crazy sometimes. And since you probably spend a lot of time around your siblings, make peace with them and try doing some of the fun things I mention below. The point is, work on building a closer relationship and have fun—laughing *with* each other, not *at* each other.

- *Be your brother's keeper...and your sister's.* The Bible says, "Carry one another's heavy loads. If you do, you will fulfill the law of Christ" (Galatians 6:2). In other words, look out for your brother and sister. Help them, support them…even defend them.

 Read Romans 12:10. Name some ways that you can live out this verse.

BOREDOM BUSTERS

Action sports—Hang out at a family spot that offers go-karts and climbing walls.

Biking—If you don't have a cool trail to ride on, set off on adventures in your neighborhood.

Cooking—Pretend you're on the Food Network and dream up some great dishes.

Dog sitting—Make some extra bucks together watching someone's pet.

ESPN—Be a kid commentator, narrating games on your street.

Fishing—Get a rod and reel and some bait and catch dinner.

Games—Pull out the board games and go old school.

Hose—Play tag with the hose in the backyard.

Igloo—Build one and see how many people can fit inside.

Junk—Gather old stuff from your attic or basement and then build something together.

King of the hill—See who rules in your neighborhood.

Launch a rocket—Buy a kit from a hobby store, build it, and then send it into orbit.

Movies—Grab some popcorn and binge-watch your favorites.

NASA—Discover their big plans for Mars.

Olympics—Host neighborhood games in your front yard.

Pool—Swim together every day.

Quit using your smartphone for a day—The person who lasts the longest is the winner.

Race—Pull out your Hot Wheels gear and have a competition.

Sugar—Make gourmet candy for your parents.

Tag—Create unusual versions of tag and invite your friends to play.

Undercover—Be spies for the afternoon.

Video game marathon—Go with a sports theme.

Water games—Fill up balloons and squirting devices and do battle.

X-games—Gather bikes and skateboards and challenge each other.

Yard—Camp out there during the summer.

Zoo—Enjoy an African safari in your town.

36

Cool Stuff to Do with Mom and Dad

I grabbed my oar and climbed into a raft with my parents, a wilderness guide, and another family we'd just met. I was ready for adventure.

My parents and I traveled to West Virginia to take on one of America's best stretches of white water: New River Gorge National River. This place lived up to its reputation!

Within minutes, my world was spinning, bouncing, and zooming in a million different directions. My nerves surged with 10,000 volts of raw fear. My heart pounded, my eyes bulged, and my vocal cords exploded with a primordial scream that was loud enough to trigger an avalanche in the Himalayas.

"YOWEEeeEEEeeeeHHHhhhEEeeLLLPPpppMEPPPppp LEEAasEEEeee!!!"

Soon the raft cruised into a calm eddy, but only for a second. The guide looked at me and winked. "That was nothing," he said and then pointed to the next plunge. "Now the fun begins!"

Suddenly, the river dropped down a twisting, narrow chute, crashing into a fury of white, foamy thunder.

"We're finished!" I told my parents. "There's no way this chintzy boat and each of our bodies can squeeze through that... AAARRRGGG—"

Tons of white water tumbled around me as the raft shot down the churning falls. Spray flew, waves crashed, and rocks jutted out at me.

"Left! Left! Left!" the guide ordered, and I began to paddle like a wild man.

The chute tore the river in two with its ragged edge of teeth. I had reached a critical point. If the raft flipped or slammed into a boulder, all of us would be finished.

"Now…right! Come on—paddle. Teamwork, everyone. *Teamwork!*"

The crew and I fought hard to stay off the rocks. It was sort of like maneuvering through a giant maze. But eventually…victory!

The raft zigzagged down the chute and plunged safely into a calm stretch of the river.

I high-fived Dad. "We're alive!"

But then the guide brought us back to reality. "Stay alert," he ordered. "This isn't Disneyland, you know!"

He was all too right. I gasped and then gripped my paddle again, ready to take on the next monster splash.

"YOWEEeeEEEeeeeHHHhhhEEee!"

◀🏈▶

My family and I are wired for adventure, especially white water rafting.

We've camped in the Rockies, explored ancient cliff dwellings in New Mexico, swum with dolphins in the Caribbean, flown over Costa Rican jungles on a zip line, biked the Golden Gate Bridge… and have rafted more times than I can remember. My favorite so far is that crazy trip through the New River Gorge.

But even better than all those adventures are the moments we spend hanging out with each other—talking, laughing…just being together. I bet you feel the same way about your family. Here's an idea: Shock your parents by taking the lead and suggesting some great things you can do together. I have a few ideas. But as you plan the fun, make it your goal to honor God by loving and encouraging each other. (That's what the Bible instructs us to do.)

WINNING WORDS

"May the God who gives endurance and encouragement give you the same attitude of mind toward each other that Christ Jesus had, so that with one mind and one voice you may glorify the God and Father of our Lord Jesus Christ" (Romans 15:5-6 NIV).

WINNING TACTICS

- *Share some crazy (kid-parent) moments.* If white water rafting isn't your thing, try something closer to home. When the weather is good, set up obstacles in the backyard and challenge your parents to a relay competition. (We did this when I was younger, and I always won!) When the weather is bad, move indoors and pull out some games (even the old-school versions that come in a box) or launch a movie marathon. Or here's something I love: Have dinner at a super special place—you know, a restaurant where they provide entertainment like jousting (Medieval Times), cliff divers (Casa Bonita in Denver), or video games (Dave and Buster's). My point is, let your imagination go wild! Be creative and have fun laughing and hanging out together. But if you decide to go white water rafting, all I can say is "YOWEEeeEEEeeeeHHHhhhEEee!"

- *Consider invading their world.* Is your dad a carpenter or a chef? Is your mom a doctor or a designer? Ask if you can step into their shoes and spend a day with them at work. Learn what drives them. Learn why they spend eight-plus hours a day doing what they do. Most important, learn how they connect with God.

- *Let them invade your world.* Catching some quality time with Mom and Dad is always the goal—and what could be better than letting them into your high-tech world? Invite them to follow you into the mysterious landscapes of *Minecraft*, *Lego Dimensions*, *Mario*, *Roblox*...or whatever game you're into. Or maybe your world gravitates toward sports, music, art, or science. Regardless of what drives you, let your parents see firsthand what captivates your imagination.

? Read 1 Thessalonians 5:9-11. How does God want us to treat others?

PRO TIP

Thomas Morstead
Serving Christ and Changing Lives

The Saints came marching in one Christmas, and New Orleans Saints punter Thomas Morstead was leading them. Morstead and an army of massive players stormed the halls of a children's hospital, passing out gifts and spreading joy to sick children.

Huge players, like Justin Drescher, Jairus Byrd, Terron Armstead, Dannell Ellerbe, Andrus Peat, and Senio Kelemete, were all laughing and having fun with the kids.

They donned their Saints jerseys and wore fuzzy red-and-white Santa hats. Cameras flashed, and smartphones recorded every conversation as the guys handed out gifts, posed for pictures, and laughed with the kids. Little did they realize the whole thing was about to go viral. The Saints' visit would quickly receive national coverage because of a series of videos that would be posted on their Facebook page.

Morstead shared what he truly lives for: sharing the love of Jesus with others.

A tip from Thomas Morstead's life: Reach out and serve others for Christ.

37

"My Family Fractured—
So What Now?"

ndless teasing. Constant humiliation. Thirteen-year-old Michael was at his breaking point. He lay on the ground by a basketball court, buckled like a crumpled Pepsi can.

"You're an absolute loser," taunted one of the boys who shoved him.

"Don't even think about shooting hoops with us," shouted another. "You don't get the game, you don't know how to play, and we're way out of your league."

Suddenly, a whistle blew, and the boys scattered, leaving Michael alone.

"What's this all about, son?" barked the school's coach.

Michael raised his head and tried to blink away the tears. "They hate me," he mumbled. "Everybody hates me 'cause I'm skinny and clumsy...and not a jock."

"Look, sports just isn't your thing," the coach responded, helping Michael to his feet. "Don't sweat the teasing. Just be a man, tough it out, and keep going."

Michael's head began to swim. *If this is manhood, then I don't want it. But I don't think I'll ever figure out how to become a man because my dad is gone. My family fractured—so what now?*

That scene happened decades ago—*way* before I was born. And the Michael in this story is the same person whose name is on the cover of this book. That's right…it's my dad! Not only did he struggle with teasing and bullying, but an even worse thing had happened to him: His own family had fractured when his mom and dad got a divorce. I can't imagine the pain he went through growing up in a broken home. Listen in on a conversation he once shared with me:

> My father abandoned my family when I was much younger than you, Christopher. I was just six when it happened. I became so sad and scared, especially as I watched my mom worry her way through what must have felt like an impossible task. She had to raise six kids all by herself! I was the youngest…and the most high-maintenance of her children.
>
> "Mrs. Ross, that boy of yours is such a worry-wart," my first-grade teacher once told her during parent-teacher conferences. Then she grabbed my mom's hand. "Is everything okay at home? How are you holding up?"
>
> I held my breath—selfishly worried that Mom would say something that would make us—actually, me— seem different…inferior. *Will my teacher stop liking us? Will the other kids think we're weird?* (As an adult, I've cut myself some slack. After all, first graders aren't supposed to worry; they're supposed to have a childhood. Sadly, I didn't.)
>
> Junior high was a nightmare. "Come on, Ross—don't be so scared of the ball," barked Mr. Battle, my PE instructor. (Yep—his name was actually *Battle*, which ironically

described the pain I endured day after day.) "Man up. Put some muscle into it." During moments like that, I would have given anything to melt into the cracks on the gym floor. *Sorry, Mr. Battle, but I don't exactly feel much like a man. Most of the time, I just feel scared.*

Can you relate to my dad's pain? Has your family been ripped apart because of divorce? If so, you're not alone. There isn't an easy way to get through the hurt, but my dad recommends a few things that can help kids work through it. Like what? Keep reading…

WINNING WORDS

"I give you peace, the kind of peace that only I can give. It isn't like the peace that this world can give. So don't be worried or afraid" (John 14:27 CEV).

WINNING TACTICS

- *We can't always control what we feel, but we can control what we do with those feelings.* First, don't be afraid of all those crazy, sad feelings inside. They are normal. *You're normal.* When really lousy things happen to us—like the divorce of our parents—we end up feeling every possible emotion: fierce anger, disappointment, deep sadness, and hopelessness. It's one thing to feel angry about our parents' divorce; it's another thing to hold on to the anger so it takes root and grows into hatred.

- *We can't rush how long it may take us to start feeling better.* Ripped-up families need time to mend. It's not like a slightly sprained ankle that we can just walk off. We need to get out of the game and give that wound some attention. We don't have to feel embarrassed or slap on a fake grin and act like everything is okay. We can be honest with ourselves and others: Divorce is lousy.

- *We can't go through this alone.* We need to talk through some of our sadness with a trusted adult—a good friend, a counselor at school, or one of our pastors at church—so we can let go of the anger. We need to let them know what's going on, not only in our houses but also in our heads.

Read Psalm 23:1-4. Who is with us when we go through hard times?

38

My Friend's Family Is Broken

*I*f God really cares, then why have all these bad things happened to me?

If God really cares, then why do I feel so alone?

If God really cares, then why is my family so messed up?

Braden jotted the questions at the top of a sheet of notebook paper—just below the title "The Worst Year of My Life!"

The stressed-out 12-year-old made a commitment to Christ at camp a few years back, but lately he wondered if God had given up on him. It was the perfect essay topic for his English assignment.

Throughout the year, a lot of bad things had happened to Braden. His parents decided it was time for a change of scenery and moved the family to a small town halfway across the state (which meant leaving his friends). Then he nearly flunked out of his new school. And worst of all, his dad walked out on his mom, little sister, and him.

Braden leaned back in his chair and squeezed his eyes shut. *God, if You really do care, I need to know it right now. I can handle a crazy move and some bad grades. But I can't deal with my parents' divorce. HELP!*

My dad and I have met a lot of kids, teens, and adults whose fractured families have caused them more pain than some people endure in a lifetime. Here's what one of those people, a guy named Mark, told us:

> My parents divorced when I was a freshman in high school, and it really hit me hard. I began to question myself as well as a lot of stuff my parents had taught me—especially their faith. I remember thinking, *Mom and Dad are Christians, but they still got a divorce. What's happening here?*
>
> My youth pastor helped me through this time and really helped me grow closer to God. Before I had my talk with my youth pastor, I had taken my questions to the wrong people, which sent me in a lot of crazy directions.

Today, Mark's life is a million times better, and his self-worth has improved too. He now cares deeply for other hurting people and even feels as if God is nudging him to tell others about the struggles his family has endured and how his faith pulled him through.

Chances are, you know people like Braden and Mark—guys and girls whose family has pulled apart or is on the brink of a breakup. They need to know that our heavenly Father will never abandon them. He won't always make our hard times easy to bear, but He will walk with us through the pain—always guiding, always comforting.

Here's a thought: Maybe you should be the one to share these comforting words with a hurting friend. If you're not sure how, I have some ideas.

WINNING WORDS

"Live under the protection
 of God Most High
 and stay in the shadow
 of God All-Powerful.
Then you will say to the LORD,
'You are my fortress,
 my place of safety;
 you are my God,
 and I trust you.'
The Lord will keep you safe
from secret traps
 and deadly diseases.
He will spread his wings
over you
 and keep you secure.
 His faithfulness is like
 a shield or a city wall"
 (Psalm 91:1-4 CEV).

WINNING TACTICS

- *Don't walk around on eggshells.* Your friend probably doesn't feel very normal right now, so he or she needs you to be normal—which means being yourself. Do the things you always do. Talk about the stuff you always talk about.

- *Be a good listener.* If your friend opens up about the pain, it's probably best not to say much at all. Just be there and listen.

- *Let your friend cry.* Don't be freaked out by a few tears and deep emotion. A grieving person needs to cry and even put their feelings into words. Encourage your buddy to talk to a trusted adult, such as your parents or a pastor.

 Read Psalm 30:5. What makes this verse so comforting?

Gabby Douglas
God First, Olympics Second

For many athletes competing in Rio, reliance on personal faith and the quest for Olympic success go hand in hand. Gymnast Gabby Douglas is certainly among those who fit into that category.

The athlete, who was first made world-famous after winning gold medals during the 2012 London Olympics, competed in 2016 in Rio as well, and her faith journey is just one of the many stories that gained attention. It's a story that was already told in depth during the 2012 Olympic season, but it's one that continues to gain traction—and with good reason. After all, Douglas was just 16 years old when she captivated the world at the London Olympics and won big.

"Faith plays a big role in my life," she says. "I don't know where I would be without it. I've always been praying for everything. And my mom always exposed me and my siblings to being a Christian and [reading] the Bible."[22]

A tip from Gabby Douglas's life: Find faith in Jesus.

39

How to Talk to Your Parents

The latest sci-fi thriller was exploding on the big screen, and I couldn't wait to see it with the guys on my football team. But there was one hugely important barrier between me and the movie—my mom!

"Hey, uh, look," I said to her. "After practice on Friday, everybody's catching a movie, and I'd...well, I'd really like to go. What do you think?"

"What's it rated?" she asked.

Suddenly, lightning flashed behind me and ominous organ music filled the room. Okay, not literally, but that's how the scene played out in my head—just as it does when I stress about upcoming tests. (Remember what happened in chapter 30?)

Actually, there was silence.

I swallowed hard and nervously shifted my eyes. I knew my mom could practically see the wheels spinning inside my head—so I had to play my cards right. *Just be cool,* I told myself. *Don't let her see you sweat.*

"Look," I said. "It has a few explosions, okay?" *Yep, she sees me sweating.* "It's not PG, and it's not suitable for little kids—I'll admit that," I continued. "But I'm not a little kid anymore. I can handle it, Mom."

She took a deep breath and folded her arms. Before I knew it, we were both deep into Media War No. 466,392…and our once-friendly discussion totally blew up.

I blurted a stinging remark—"You *never* care about what I want; you're just out to drive me crazy all the time!"—followed by a long list of gripes…like the time when I was 12 months old and my mom took away my favorite squeaky toy and made me eat strained asparagus! (Once again, I'm exaggerating, but my point is, I was mad!)

By the end of the night, the battle was growing even more intense—and nothing was getting resolved.

If you're tired of pointless arguments with Mom and Dad that seem to get nowhere—except maybe you being grounded and sent to your room—try these three winning strategies for better conversations. (I learned them from my parents, and they work.)

Begin with Scripture first and then dive in. Maybe consider taping verses to your bedroom wall (or your forehead) and memorizing them. They'll help you connect with your parents, say what's on your mind—and possibly even get your way.

WINNING WORDS

"As God's chosen people, holy and dearly loved, clothe yourselves with compassion, kindness, humility, gentleness and patience. Bear with each other and forgive one another if any of you has a grievance against someone. Forgive as the Lord forgave you. And over all these virtues

put on love, which binds them all together in perfect unity"
(Colossians 3:12-14 NIV).

WINNING TACTICS

- *Remember that attitude is everything.* When Mom and Dad
  tick you off, never fire back with an angry remark. This only
  raises defenses and widens the gap. A controlled temper and
  respectful tone allow for a better chance to deflate the conflict.

- *Stay away from blanket statements.* Saying stuff like "You
  never," "You always," and "You don't ever" make it sound like
  you're blaming your parents. Instead, share your feelings by
  saying *I* first. For example, begin with "I want" or "I feel."

- *Communicate using "shared meaning."* Here's how it
  works:

  1. You're bugged that you can't see a movie with your
     friends, so you approach Mom and Dad and say,
     "Could we talk about this? I'd like you to hear my side."

  2. Once they agree to hear you out, you explain your point
     of view, which you've thought through ahead of time.

  3. Next, Mom and Dad repeat what they heard you say.

  4. You then clarify what they said, making sure they heard
     you accurately.

  5. The conversation continues with your parents sharing
     their point of view and you listening and repeating what
     they said.

The goal of shared meaning is to be heard accurately. Once
you've had a chance to state your case and listen to theirs,

the moment is set for communication—not pointless battles that go nowhere.

 Read Proverbs 29:20. Why is it important to choose our words carefully?

40

How to Pray with Your Family

It was the day of my basketball tryouts, and I was nervous. My stomach hurt, but I couldn't eat…and I had a whole bunch of thoughts inside that I wanted to share but just couldn't get out. Instead, I felt like a jumbled mass of panic, fear, and irritation. Everything bugged me, and none of it made sense.

"How are you feeling?" my mom asked me over and over, even as we stepped into my school's gym.

"Mom—please stop asking," I said. "I just don't…well, I just can't. Please, please just stop making me talk!"

I know my parents meant well, but like I said, I just couldn't get the words out or think straight. My brain had zeroed in on the tryouts.

My dad put his hand on my shoulder and whispered, "Let's pray."

I shrugged it off. "NO, Dad—not here, not in front of everyone." If I was too nervous to talk, how on earth could I pray?

"It's okay," Dad assured me. "We'll step into the hallway, and we'll find a quiet spot. I promise—prayer will help."

I reluctantly agreed, and my parents did all the praying. I just listened.

"Lord God, please calm Christopher's nerves," Dad prayed. "Help him to do his best. Help him to have peace whether or not he makes the team. Amen."

I hugged my family and then headed onto the court.

Praying really helped that day—and in the days that followed. I didn't make the team, but knowing that God was at my side gave me courage, and talking freely to Him helped me to handle the disappointment I felt. (Flip back to chapter 5 to learn what I went through.)

Even though it was hard at first, the Lord gave me peace and helped me to know that everything was okay. A few weeks later, I was picked to wrestle and eventually to play football.

Want to know how to pray with your family, your friends, your team...and anyone you meet? It really isn't that hard. There aren't any secrets to learn or formulas to follow. We don't have to make big speeches. (Actually, God doesn't want our speeches; He wants to hear our hearts.) All we have to do is focus on Jesus and talk to Him. In fact, Jesus knows everything about prayer and shows us how to do it.

In the Bible, we quickly learn that prayer was practically the breath Jesus breathed, something He did every day and all the time, and an important way to be close to God. Jesus modeled a perfect prayer life, and He encouraged His followers to never stop praying.

"When you pray, go into a room alone and close the door. Pray to your Father in private. He knows what is done in private, and he will reward you. When you pray, don't talk on and on as people do who don't know God. They think God likes to hear long prayers" (Matthew 6:6-7 CEV).

WINNING WORDS

"Once Jesus was in a certain place praying. As he finished, one of his disciples came to him and said, 'Lord, teach us to pray, just as John taught his disciples.'

Jesus said, 'This is how you should pray:
'Father, may your name be kept holy.
    May your Kingdom come soon.
Give us each day the food we need,
and forgive us our sins,
    as we forgive those who sin against us.
And don't let us yield to temptation'"
    (Luke 11:1-4 NLT).

WINNING TACTICS

- *Know what prayer is.* Prayer is not just going through the motions, saying a bunch of thoughtless, mechanical words—as some people do when they give thanks for a meal. It is actually communicating with the one and only eternal God. Jesus is our best friend, and He wants us to tell Him about everything that's going on in our lives. He wants to know the desires of our heart, how badly we feel when we fail, how happy we are when good things happen—everything!

- *Don't hold back—just do it!* So many of my friends say things like "I don't know what to say" or "I don't know how to pray!" Actually, I've said that too. But here's what I'm learning: If we've figured out how to talk on the phone or Snapchat or text, then we know how to pray.

- *Think of stuff to pray about.* Even though prayer involves talking, which most of us are pretty good at, I'll admit that it's sometimes hard to pray with our families. We get tired, distracted, busy, and even a little embarrassed. It can be awkward praying with our parents and our siblings. In the Bible, Jesus's closest friends couldn't stay focused as He prayed in the Garden of Gethsemane. (See Matthew 26:36-46). Jesus was distressed as He prayed that night. Three times He came back to His friends to find them asleep. So let's cut ourselves a break. We're normal! It's not just a struggle for modern-day kids and their families; people have always had obstacles as they try to draw closer to God. That's why I think you're going to like the game plan my dad and I put together. (See below.)

? Read 2 Chronicles 7:13-16. If we pray and seek God, what does He promise?

KICK-STARTING MY FAMILY PRAYER TIME

Here's something that works for my family. During each family prayer time, we choose a word that describes who God is to us, and then we look for Bible verses that use that word. We end by praying about the topic...and for each other.

Here are seven topics to get you started. Once you've prayed through these, be creative and come up with a bunch more on your own. The important thing is to start praying as a family.

God is...

Alpha and Omega
Read Revelation 22:13.

- *As a family*: Talk about what *alpha* and *omega* mean. Discuss what Jesus means when He says He is the "Alpha and the Omega."

- *What to pray about*: Thank God for His goodness and for giving us life. Thank God for families.

All-Knowing
Read Psalm 139:2.

- *As a family*: Using this passage as a conversation starter, ask these questions: "Since God is all-knowing, is it okay to be completely honest with Him about our hurts, doubts, and fears? What might you have a hard time being completely honest with God about?"

- *What to pray about*: Thank God for caring about every detail of our lives. Ask Him to bless everyone in your family.

Everywhere
Read Psalm 139:7-8.

- *As a family*: Knowing that God is everywhere all at once, talk about how it makes you feel when you go to school or camp or on vacation.

- *What to pray about*: Thank God for being everywhere and ask Him to help you know that He is with you wherever you go.

Forgiving
Read 1 John 1:9.

- *As a family*: Talk about how Jesus Christ paid the penalty for our sins and invites us to live forever with Him.

- *What to pray about*: Thank Jesus for dying on the cross and giving us eternal life with Him, and tell the Lord that you are sorry for messing up at times.

Loving
Read 1 John 4:7.

- *As a family*: Talk about the different kinds of love we feel: for pizza, for our pets, for each other, for God. How are they different? Describe God's love for us.

- *What to pray about*: Thank Jesus for being the source of all true love, and ask the Lord for help as you reach out to others.

A Peacemaker
Read Matthew 5:9.

- *As a family*: Take turns sharing why it's important for each member of your family to live in peace with each other and with God.

- *What to pray about*: Ask God to give your family peace and to protect you from turmoil.

Trustworthy
Read Isaiah 26:4.

- *As a family*: Talk about how God sees and honors the faith of every member of your family. Is the Lord trustworthy in all situations?

- *What to pray about*: Thank Jesus for His dependability, and ask the Lord to help your family trust God in all situations.

PRO TIP

Darrell Waltrip
The Ultimate Victory Lane

Engines roared like B-52 bombers awaiting takeoff.

Drivers sat on the grid, watching for the green light. One of those men of thunder was a legend on the NASCAR circuit—No. 17, Darrell Waltrip. (Remember the character Darrell Cartrip in Disney's *Cars* series? That's him!)

After countless runs on the oval track, Darrell throttled his 650-horsepowered Chevrolet into the winner's circle at the Super Bowl of stock car racing events: the prestigious Daytona 500. He's a three-time NASCAR Cup Series champion.

Today, he's a motorsports analyst, national TV broadcaster, and a voice actor. Looking back, he firmly believes his faith has pulled him through a number of hard times. "Some of the toughest times came after I gave my life to the Lord," Waltrip says. "When I was injured, it was hard sitting out races. But I had the Lord to turn to. If I didn't, it might have been the end of my career. God is always there—during the good times as well as the bad."[23]

A tip from Darrell Waltrip's life: Turn to God when life is hard.

MY ALL-STAR STATS ABOUT FAMILY LIFE

Describe your "home team."

What makes your family champions? What would get you off a losing streak?

_____

_____

_____

_____

Evaluate your coaches—Mom and Dad.

Have their calls been fair? Why or why not?

_____

_____

_____

_____

Jot some thoughts about sibling competition.

What would improve game time with your family?

_____

_____

_____

_____

Notes

1. Mary Fairchild, "Allyson Felix: Christian Athlete Profile," *ThoughtCo* (blog), March 24, 2017, https://www.thoughtco.com/allyson-felix-biography-700345.

2. "Mark Sanchez: Five Increase Questions," *The Increase* (blog), 2018, https://theincrease .com/author/mark-sanchez/.

3. From an interview conducted for Michael Ross, Lee Warren, and the *Breakaway* team, "*Breakaway*'s All-Star Series," *Breakaway*, May 2006, 22.

4. From an interview conducted for Michael Ross, Rick Houston, and the *Breakaway* team, "The Fast and the Faithful," *Breakaway*, August 2008, 28.

5. From an interview conducted for Michael Ross, Jeremy V. Jones, and the *Breakaway* team, "The Fast and the Faithful," *Breakaway*, August 2008, 27.

6. Jeremy V. Jones, *Walking on Water: The Spirituality of the World's Top Surfers* (Ventura, CA: Regal, 2006), 22.

7. From an interview conducted for Michael and Tiffany Ross, *Faith That Breathes* (Uhrichsville, OH: Barbour, 2004), 288.

8. From an interview conducted for Michael Ross, "Plugged In Devotion," *Breakaway*, August 1991, 19-20.

9. Jon Ackerman, "Philadelphia Eagles Give "Glory to God" After Winning Super Bowl LII," Sports Spectrum, February 5, 2018, https://sportsspectrum.com/sport/football/2018/02/05/ philadelphia-eagles-give-glory-god-winning-super-bowl-lii/.

10. Mike Yorkey, *Playing with Purpose* (Uhrichsville, OH: Barbour, 2012), 109.

11. Patrick Dunn, "Team Faith," *Breakaway*, February 2009, 21-22.

12. Elisabeth Freeman, "Living My Dream," *Christianity Today*, https://www.christianitytoday .com/iyf/truelifestories/interestingpeople/17.13.html.

13. Mike Yorkey, *Tim Tebow* (Uhrichsville, OH: Barbour, 2012), 131.

14. From an interview with James Dobson, *Focus on the Family*, 2002.

15. Greg Hartman, "Rugby by God's Rules," *Breakaway*, October 2007, 11-12.

16. Jordan Sheppard, "As a Christian, NBA Star Kevin Durant Remains Humble," *God Reports* (blog), February 20, 2017, http://blog.godreports.com/2017/02/as-a-christian-nba-star-kevin -durant-remains-humble/.

17. Stacey Lee, "Ed Carpenter Is on the Fast Track," *Breakaway*, May 2007, 21.

18. Interview conducted by Michael Ross.

19. "Olympic Gymnast Simone Biles on Faith and Courage," *The 700 Club*, 2018, https:// www1.cbn.com/olympic-gymnast-simone-biles-faith-and-courage.

20. Adapted from Chad Bonham, "A Conversation with U.S. Women's Soccer Team Member

Tobin Heath," *Beliefnet* (blog), December 2011, http://www.beliefnet.com/columnists/inspiringathletes/2011/12/a-conversation-with-u-s-womens-world-cup-soccer-team-member-tobin-heath.html.

21. Chad Bonham, "A Conversation with U.S. Olympian Kendrick Farris," *Beliefnet* (blog), June 2012, http://www.beliefnet.com/columnists/inspiringathletes/2012/06/a-conversation-with-u-s-olympian-kendrick-farris.html#By2lXesYEsQZWDOf.99.

22. Billy Hallowell, "U.S. Olympian Gabby Douglas' Intense Christian Faith and Its Profound Role in Her Quest for Success," *Deseret News Faith*, August 10, 2016, https://www.deseretnews.com/article/865659764/US-Olympian-Gabby-Douglas-intense-Christian-faith-2-and-its-profound-role-in-her-quest-for.html.

23. From a personal interview with Michael Ross.

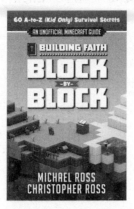

Improve Your Game, Build Your Faith

Decisions, decisions. In both the virtual world and the real world, you have to make a bunch of choices. Mess up in the virtual world of Minecraft and you can always start over. But in the real world, where the decisions you make have *real* consequences, both good and bad, it's not that simple.

Where can you go for help? Is there a gamer's guide for living? Yes, it's called the Bible—and God created it to help you win!

Join gamer Dragee90 as he shares daily devotions packed with secrets to success in two key areas of your life:

- **Gameplay**—Learn A-to-Z tips and tricks for virtual world-building and secrets and online survival in the game of Minecraft.

- **Real Life**—Dragee90 reveals some of his own daily struggles and gives you powerful Scripture verses from the Bible you can use to overcome life's biggest obstacles.

Building faith block by block is easy when you start with the right foundation!

To learn more about Harvest House books and
to read sample chapters, visit our website:

www.harvesthousepublishers.com

HARVEST HOUSE PUBLISHERS
EUGENE, OREGON